Maritime Forces in Pursuit of National Security

Policy Imperatives for India

Maritime Forces in Pursuit of National Security

Policy Imperatives for India

Commander Gurpreet S Khurana

Institute for Defence Studies and Analyses
New Delhi

SHIPRA

Views expressed are of the author and not necessarily of the IDSA.

ISBN: 978-81-7541-430-3

First Published in India in 2008

Maritime Forces in Pursuit of National Security: Policy Imperatives for India

Published by:
SHIPRA PUBLICATIONS
115-A, Vikas Marg, Shakarpur, Delhi-110092, INDIA
Phone: 91-11-65277210, 91-11-22500954
Fax: 91-11-22458662
E-mail: info@shiprapublications.com
www.shiprapublications.com

Contents

Preface

It is well known that *National Security* represents the overall security of a state in terms of its core values and varied interests and the strategy to achieve it flows from the state's *Vision and Objectives*. India's National Security Strategy has not yet been formally articulated. Nonetheless, it can be extrapolated with reasonable clarity from the growth trajectory of its Comprehensive National Power (CNP) and its growing eminence among nations in almost every facet of consequence: military economic, technological, industrial and human development.

Restricted to the realm of the oceans, *Maritime Security* is a 'subset' of National Security, but it also relates to a very wide spectrum of national interests. At one end are those linked to civilian facets like mercantile trade, shipbuilding, resource exploitation, law-enforcement and preservation of marine environment. At the other extreme, are the military-strategic dimensions to preserve the state's survival interests. A state's ability to use the sea to further these interests is reckoned in terms of its *Maritime Power*, of which, *Naval power* is the key constituent. In this monograph, the term *Naval Power* encompasses the aggregate capabilities of the maritime security forces charged with functions ranging from military combat to law-enforcement at sea; and further on, from safety of people engaged in maritime activities at sea, to preserving the marine environment.

Given the global phenomenon of national interests shifting towards the oceans, maritime security has already assumed immense worldwide significance. This is extremely pertinent to

India, whose stakes are rapidly expanding beyond its terrestrial confines in consonance with its growing CNP. As a corollary, those who seek to contain India's rising influence or hurt it in any way are more likely to target its vital interests at sea or in the littoral. How does this translate into an increased responsibility for India's maritime forces? How has the task-domain of these forces expanded from traditional 'hard' security (in conjunction with land and air forces) to 'softer' issues like economic and environmental security that are closely linked to the use of oceans. Furthermore, owing to their intrinsic attributes, can sea-borne forces be expected to satiate national security interests beyond the ambit of maritime security? What attributes of these forces could enable this? These queries need to be objectively addressed.

This book examines the maritime security and strategic concerns that confront India in context of Asia's geo-strategic environment. The setting also encompasses the interests of all 'players' operating in the regional systemic. The aim is two-fold; first to deduce the extent to which India's naval power can meet national (including maritime) security challenges and secondly, to review the salient imperatives for India's employment of maritime forces to meet contemporary challenges.

Academicians and practitioners have written extensively on India's maritime history and asserted the imperative of developing its naval power. Many of these writings also recount Indian Navy's operations in the past, drawing attention to their successes or the lessons learnt from their failures. Instructive and valuable in own right, these also serve as an indicator of India's naval strategy, but are not specifically directed at examining its security challenges and its response strategy. Besides, the altered regional geo-political and security scenario; since the end of Cold War; has placed new demands on maritime forces in terms of their structures and operational tasks; thereby redefining the erstwhile concept of "naval strategy" to be extended beyond its erstwhile purely military connotation to include all other functions of naval power to safeguard national security imperatives.

In India, official documents on security policies and doctrinal issues have always been scarce. It was only in April 2004 that the *Indian Maritime Doctrine* provided an insight into India's naval strategy. Thereafter in 2007, the *Freedom of the Seas: India's Military Maritime Strategy* was India's first official articulation to be made available in the public domain. It was, therefore, fortuitous for this book to draw upon the contents of these two publications. The work in hand is a modest attempt at a more detailed and specific examination of the key security issues mentioned in these official documents, for which India will need to employ its naval power. However, as indicated earlier, this book is broader in scope since it conceptualises the term 'naval power' to encompass the collective capacity of *all* maritime forces, viz. not only navy, but also coast guard and marine police of the coastal (provincial) states.

This work is intended for a wide-spectrum readership. At one end is a layman questing for a greater awareness of maritime security affairs of India - a country that has cast away its inward-oriented moorings to realize its vital stakes in and across the ocean realm. At the other end, it is meant to be an input for the concerned government officials for policy making. It also addresses the academics, scholars and 'think-tanks' who bear an important influence on state policies.

This writing does not necessarily reflect views of the Institute for Defence Studies and Analyses (IDSA) or the Indian Navy.

I am indebted to the anonymous referees for their valuable comments and suggestions, which I have incorporated in this work to the best of my ability.

Gurpreet S Khurana
Commander
Research Fellow

IDSA, New Delhi
January 2008

List of Maps

Map No.

List of Photographs

Photograph No.

Abbreviations

A&N	-	Andaman and Nicobar Islands
ASEAN	-	Association of South East Asian Nations
ASW	-	Anti Submarine Warfare
CBG	-	Carrier Battle Group
CBM	-	Confidence Building Measure
C^4ISR	-	Command, Control, Communications, Computers, Intelligence, Surveillance and Reconnaissance
CSI	-	Container Security Initiative
DRDO	-	Defence Research and Development Organisation
EEZ	-	Exclusive Economic Zone
FAC	-	Fast Attack Craft
FoC	-	Flags of Convenience (shipping)
IPKF	-	Indian Peace-keeping Force
IOR	-	Indian Ocean Region
ISI	-	Inter Services Intelligence (Pakistan)
JMSDF	-	Japan Maritime Self Defence Force
LACM	-	Land Attack Cruise Missile
LCS	-	Legal Continental Shelf
LCU	-	Landing Craft Utility

LNG	-	Liquefied Natural Gas
LPD	-	Landing Platform Dock
LST	-	Landing Ship Tank
LTTE	-	Liberation Tigers of Tamil Eelam
MCM	-	Mine Counter-measures
MDA	-	Maritime Domain Awareness
NEWN	-	Navy Enterprise Wide Network
OOA	-	Out of Area (operations)
PLA	-	People's Liberation Army (PRC)
PSI	-	Proliferation Security Initiative
SAR	-	Search and Rescue (operations)
SSN	-	Nuclear-propelled submarine
SSBN	-	Nuclear-propelled Ballistic-missile submarine
UAV	-	Unmanned Aerial Vehicle
UN/ UNO	-	United Nations (Organisation)
UNCLOS-3	-	Third United Nations Convention for Laws of the Sea, 1982
WMD	-	Weapon of Mass Destruction

CHAPTER 1

Introduction

Historical Backdrop

Ancient literature and artifacts provide ample historical evidence of India's rich maritime traditions and seafaring activities during the Indus Valley civilization dating back to about 3,000 BC. The world's first tidal dock for building ships was built at Lothal port in the present-day Indian state of Gujarat in about 2,500 BC, i.e. around the time when the first western civilization was born. One finds a mention of nautical skills and even naval expeditions in the Indian *Vedic* mythology of 2,000 BC. Vivid accounts are available of large seagoing ships having been built by the *Maurya* dynasty (4th to 2nd century BC), and its overseas commercial intercourse with lands as far away as the present-day Greece and Libya. Navigational aids like the magnetic compass (*Matsya Yantra*[1]) are known to have been first used in India in 4th or 5th century AD. Indian astronomers like Aryabhatta and Varahamihira mapped the positions of celestial bodies in the 6th century AD, thereby developing a method to compute the ship's position with reference to these bodies.

While trade had been the predominant maritime activity, in the earlier part of the *Hindu*-period, Indian kingdoms like the Cholas (985-1054 AD) also developed naval power to embark on religious, cultural and colonizing missions to Sri Lanka and eastwards as far way as Japan. However, the period 11th century onwards witnessed a steady decay of naval might due to rivalry and ensuing sea-battles amongst the kingdoms. By the time they were challenged by the Portuguese at sea in the early 16th century, the Indians totally lost command of the seas, which is often stated to be the principal cause of India's subjugation by the major naval powers of the West.[2]

During the British colonial rule, India's naval defence was the responsibility of the Royal Navy (RN), with the Royal Indian Navy (RIN) being its mere adjunct tasked for coastal defence. When India attained independence in August 1947 plans were drawn up for a balanced navy with adequate force levels in consonance with its vast maritime interests. However, the Indian Navy eventually turned out to be merely a shadow of what was envisaged. This occurred due to various reasons, including the fact that the plans did not fit into the strategic calculus of the British.

Later in the 1950s and 1960s, India's political leaders realized the dangers of being weak at sea. The famous words of Jawaharlal Nehru, the first prime-minister, became indelible in India's naval history,

> *"Now that we are free, we have once again reiterated the importance of the sea. We cannot afford to be weak at sea ... history has shown that whatever power controls the Indian Ocean has, in the first instance, India's sea-borne trade at her mercy, and in the second, India's very independence itself."*[3]

This realization was accompanied with a vision to

resurrect India's naval power, but this could not be achieved due to adverse circumstances, primarily in terms of limited resources and overland military threats from Pakistan and China. India's inability to look seawards during those decades was a serious omission of two imperatives, which acted to its detriment. *Firstly*, by not building naval power, New Delhi failed to cater for consequences of the progressive attenuation of British naval power east of the Suez, which began with the end of the second World War .[4] This led to increase of superpower activity in these waters by end-1960s during Cold War, with attendant security ramifications for India. *Secondly*, the lofty mountain ranges stretching across India's northern frontiers always presented a nearly insurmountable barrier to its land communications for trade. A greater emphasis on maritime/ naval power would have been invaluable supplement to the process of India's economic development. In addition to these adversities, the lack of maritime recourse to national security, over the years, led to etching of a continental outlook in the minds of policymakers. This resulted in the non-perception of a broader global picture and lack of a strategic orientation amongst them.

The 1971 Indo-Pak War was a watershed in India's naval history, which reinforced the potential of naval power and which led to an increased desire amongst the Indian leadership to acquire it. The successful naval operations during the war, and particularly the blockade and innovative missile-boat attacks on Karachi harbour,[5] validated the navy's utility, even in support of a land battle. On the other hand, the US naval coercion during the war though the deployment of its carrier task force in Indian Ocean demonstrated India's vulnerability and reinforced the imperative for naval deterrence.

Another factor for a greater consideration of maritime

security issues in India during the 1970s was the ongoing process of international deliberations for the *United Nations Convention for Laws of the Sea* (UNCLOS), which was later finalized in 1982. The UNCLOS was expected to bestow on coastal states the jurisdiction over extensive maritime zones for economic exploitation. The need for a dedicated sea-borne security force with law enforcement powers led to the formation of the Indian Coast Guard in August 1978. This also led to significant naval acquisitions; first to cater for the impending spatial increase of responsibilities till the Coast Guard was self-sufficient to discharge its role, and secondly, due to the possibility of some maritime neighbours asserting their claims militarily, like what had occurred in the South China Sea (the Sino-Vietnamese conflict over Paracel Islands in 1974).

The latter half of the 1980s was very favourable for India's naval power. *First*, the period witnessed an induction of potent naval/ power-projection platforms such as the second aircraft carrier (INS *Viraat*), the nuclear submarine (INS *Chakra*) and long-range maritime patrol aircraft (TU-142). This was primarily driven by the need to deter the US, since the strengthening of its strategic relationship with Pakistan was perceived as inimical to India. *Secondly*, the Indian leadership was more amenable to the use of military power overseas, which included the 1987 peacekeeping operations in Sri Lanka (Operation *Pawan*) and the 1988 assistance to Maldives to overcome the attempted coup (Operation *Cactus*). Paradoxically, however, the augmentation of naval capabilities caused greater apprehensions of India's intentions in the regional neighbourhood (in countries as far away as Australia), rather than its actual use (In fact, the latter was largely approved by the global community). This was primarily because the material growth of the Indian Navy was not accompanied by sufficient efforts at transparency and trust-building with India's immediate and extended maritime neighbourhood.

The momentum of India's naval growth was not sustained in the following decade. The 1990s witnessed a dwindling of force levels due to the financial crisis and the resulting reduced monetary allocation for defence. Besides, the disintegration of the Soviet Union caused a disruption in the supply of spare-parts; and considering that nearly 70 per cent of naval platforms were of Soviet origin, it severely affected operational capabilities of the navy. The capability void was magnified with the entering into force of the UNCLOS in November 1994 and the addition of an extensive sea area to India's existing maritime zone (the territorial waters). Plans for the Coast Guard, to assume all constabulary tasks in the area could not fructify due to severe force level constraints; a void that continues to this day.

Since the late-1990s however, the country has steered a steady course towards acquiring naval power. Besides, there has been a palpable 'reorientation' in New Delhi's policy since the mid-1990s, primarily on two counts. The first is in terms of the increasing use of the navy as an instrument of foreign policy and its efforts to build "bridges of friendship" across the seas in the regional neighbourhood and beyond. The government decision in 2006, to create a Flag rank at the Integrated Headquarters of the Ministry of Defence (Navy), entrusted with 'Foreign Cooperation'[6] is among the many indicators. The second is the increasing frequency employment of naval power for the security of Indians abroad and protecting their legitimate interests, which significantly, is also stated in the Indian Maritime Doctrine.[7] These issues are discussed at length in the following chapters.

Current Geo-Strategic Setting

The end of Cold War led to unipolar world, accompanied with uncertainties and a sort of fluidity in the geo-political and security environment. While unfolding of events so far has not generated much optimism in terms of global peace and security, many are unsure whether the emergence of a multi-polar world order would be positive either. The region, wherein most insecurity prevails, is in the 'arc of instability' stretching from West Asia to north-east Asia. It is true that the likelihood of major armed conflicts has declined over the years due to increased focus of states on obtaining dividends from globalization and their reduced obsession over issues of 'territoriality'. Exceptions however exist, and more so in the maritime domain. As land resources deplete, the attention of states is being increasingly drawn towards the prevailing contentions over maritime zones, and linked to it, their claims over islands. This is leading states to pay a greater attention to enhancing their naval (and in some cases power-projection) capabilities, and thereby increasing the potential for conflicts at sea. Added to these insecurities are the ominous contours of sub-conventional threats, like organised crime and notably, terrorism being resorted to by separatists and religious fundamentalists. The larger Asian region and its maritime space – in other words, the Indo-Pacific region – is likely, therefore, to continue as an arena of competition and conflict.

Of greater applicability to India is the Indian Ocean,[8] whose historic importance has prevailed well into the present times.[9] Its current geo-strategic significance essentially lies in maritime communications – its *shipping routes* for international merchandise trade and commerce, and in military context, the *sea-lines of communication* (SLOC) for strategic imports and military mobility. The two are hereinafter clubbed under the term *sea-lines*, with the key stretches depicted in Map 1.

Since the Indian Ocean is virtually locked by the arching of the Asian landmass in its north, the relatively restricted ocean space makes its sea-lines critical for any sea-borne movement from west to east and vice versa. Even in late-1990s, when only one-fifth of the trade flow through the Ocean was intra-regional, it was more than either the Atlantic or the Pacific oceans.[10] By 2020, when Asia accounts for 60 per cent of global GDP, the attendant increase in trade would add to mercantile flows substantially. The Indian Ocean sea-lines are particularly relevant for access to fossil-fuel reservesof West Asia, which is known to hold 65 percent of the world's oil and 35 percent of its gas (the Myanmar–Bangladesh area has now become a notable supplement). Of the 200 merchant ships transiting Indian Ocean every day, 40 per cent are tankers. The criticality of these imports for the energy-hungry economies of Asia-Pacific brings forth the vitality of the sea-line extending from Persian Gulf to East Asia and passing through two principal maritime choke points – *Strait of Hormuz* and *Straits of Malacca and Singapore* (See Map 1). Some analysts therefore aptly call it the 'New Silk Route'.[11] Other important sea-lines from the East and West also merge with this strategic route.

Some analysts even go to the extent of attributing the increased salience of Indian Ocean to the 'rise' of India. Donald Berlin, of Asia-Pacific Centre for Security Studies (Honolulu), adds that "New Delhi's (increasing) interest in affairs of this Ocean…will be accompanied by a growing interest by others – especially major states – in these waters, either to check India or to ally with it".[12] The *Tsunami* experience also validates India's growing awareness of its normative role in its maritime environs.

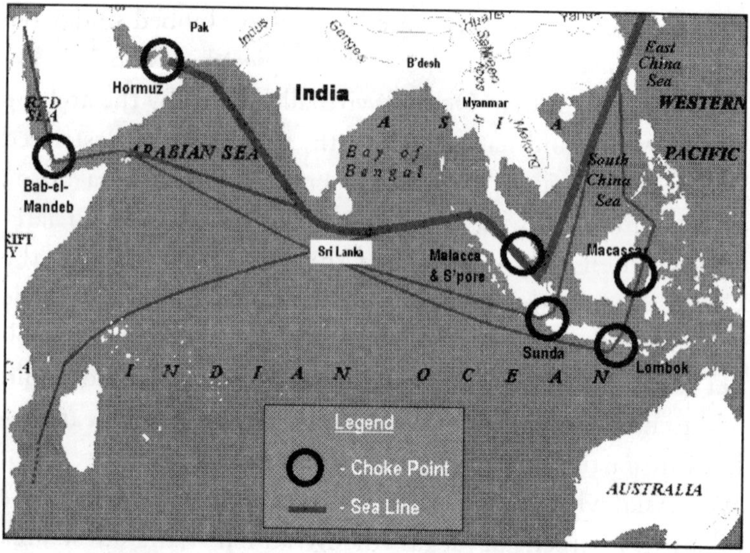

Source: Cdr GS Khurana

Map 1: Indian Ocean and its Principal Sea-lines

During the disaster-relief operation, the global community took keen notice of the naval powers, that were both *committed* and *capable* of reacting to such eventualities. India stood out amongst them due to its prompt response and the ability to provide succour to three of its neighbours despite having been among the worst affected itself.

REFERENCES

1. Literally, 'fish-machine'. It was a magnetized-iron fish made to float on oil to indicate the northerly direction.
2. R Adm (Retd.) Satyindra Singh. Blueprint to Bluewater. *Lancer*, New Delhi, 1992, pp. 4-11.
3. Address by Pranab Mukherjee, Defence Minister of India, titled, 'India's Strategic Perspective' at The Carnegie Endowment For International Peace, June 27, 2005, Washington DC, at http://

www.carnegieendowment.org/files/Mukherjee_Transcript_06-27-051.pdf p. 3 (Accessed 01 Jul 07).

4. In the mid-1950s, the same was later propagated by the US as the "Vacuum Theory" to rationalize the entry of its own military forces into the Indian Ocean. See, Nandhini Iyer. *India and the Indian Ocean*. ABC Publishers, 1983, p. 46.
5. V. Adm (Retd.) Mihir K. Roy. War in the Indian Ocean. *Lancer*, 1995, pp. 219-243.
6. Rajat Pandit, 'Navy Gears Up to Tackle Strategic Challenges', *Times of India*, September 12, 2005, p. 13.
7. Indian Maritime Doctrine, Integrated Headquarters, Ministry of Defence (Navy), April 25, 2004, p. 59.
8. In this book, the term "Indian Ocean" is inclusive of its contiguous seas (from Red Sea to Andaman Sea) and adjoining choke points (from the Suez Canal to the straits of Southeast Asia).
9. Devendra Kaushik. *Perspectives on Security in the Indian Ocean Region*. Allied Publishers, 1987, pp. 7-19.
10. N.N. Vohra, 'Security in the Indian Ocean: An Overview', in Jasjit Singh (ed.), *Bridges Across the Indian Ocean*, IDSA publication, New Delhi, June 1997, p. 20.
11. C. Uday Bhaskar, "Regional Naval Cooperation", IDSA *Strategic Analysis*, Vol. 15(8), November 1992, p. 736.
12. Donald Berlin, "Indian Ocean Redux", *Journal of the Indian Ocean Studies*, Vol. 10(1), April 2002, p. 28.

CHAPTER 2

India's Maritime Interests

The Indian Maritime Doctrine (2004) states that the Indian Ocean Region (IOR) is India's area of maritime-strategic interest.[1] The Indian Ocean is the only ocean in the world to bear a country's name, but it is important to India for reasons beyond mere etymology. Besides India's location, its geographical disposition and peninsular shape make its waters virtually contiguous to India's landmass. This chapter examines India's interest in this maritime space of immense significance.

Maritime Zones

In November 1994, UNCLOS bestowed states the right to harness maritime resources in their *Exclusive Economic Zones* (EEZ) extending up to 200 nm seawards from the coast. Owing to India's long coastline (the fifteenth longest in the world stretching 7,500 km) and widespread island territories, India gets an extensive EEZ of 2.2 million square km; that is nearly two-thirds of its land area (See Map 2). Besides, a *Legal Continental Shelf* (LCS) up to 350 nm from the coast would be added after India submits its claim by May 13, 2009, which is likely to provide an additional seabed area of about 1.5 million sq km for economic exploitation. The total area under India's maritime jurisdiction may then even exceed its terrestrial space of about 3 million sq km.

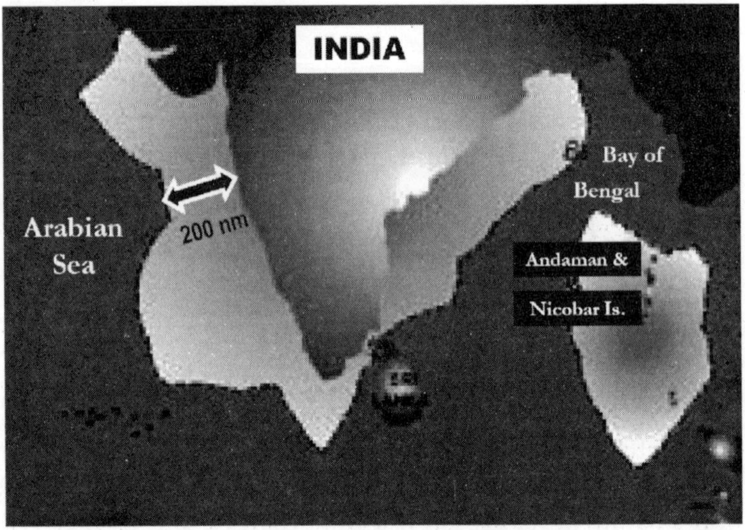

Source: National Institute of Oceanography (NIO)

Map 2: India's Exclusive Economic Zone

These maritime zones are known to hold an immense wealth of natural resources like fossil fuels, minerals and fish stock. About two-third of India's domestic production of crude oil and natural gas comes from here (See Map 3). The future potential of these offshore locations is also high considering the 'encouraging' response of Indian, and even some foreign companies to the exploration acreages offered by the government.[2] India's offshore resources are presently sourced from Bombay High relatively closer to the western coast (up to a maximum of about 200 km) and the various river basins off eastern coast, such as Krishna-Godavari, Cauvery and Mahanadi. In the coming years, extraction rigs are likely to be sited much further away from the coast (including in LCS) as new discoveries are made with improved technologies, and as deep-water extraction becomes more cost effective. Besides, prospective areas

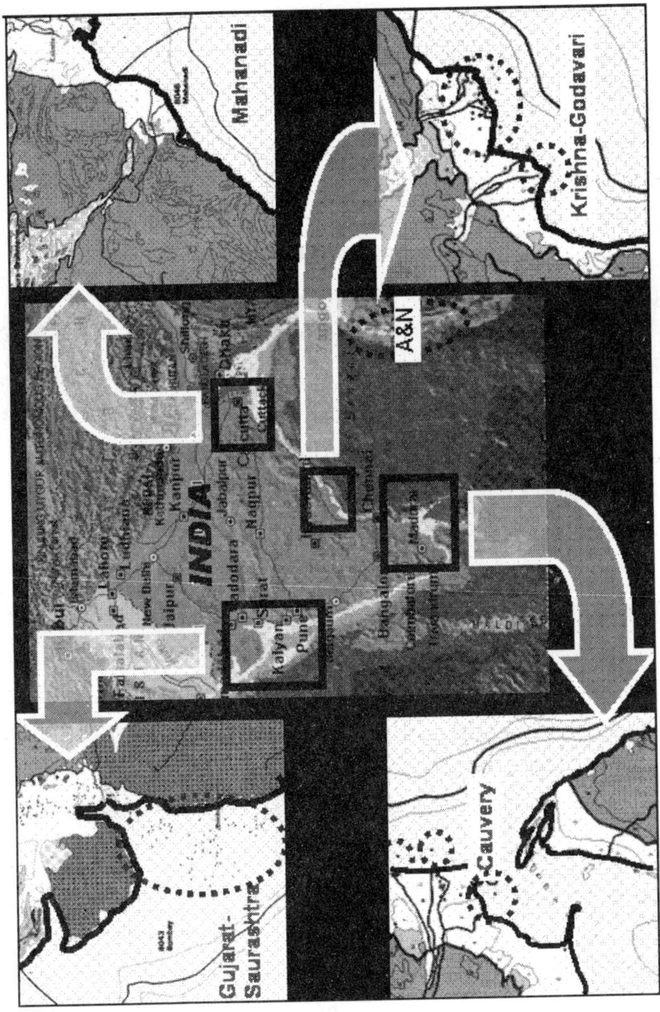

Map 3: India's Offshore Oil and Gas Fields

Source: Cdr GS Khurana

have been identified off India's far-flung island territories. While the Laccadive/Lakshadweep ridge (Arabian Sea) contains natural gas hydrates, the sea areas off Andaman and Nicobar Islands (located 1,200 km from the mainland) are known to possess the largest reserves of Coal Bed Methane (CBM) in the country.[3]

In the future, India will also turn to extraction of seabed minerals as and when it becomes economically viable. In 1987, India was accorded a "pioneer investor" status by the International Seabed Authority (ISBA) under UNCLOS and allotted an area of 1,50,000 sq km in the central Indian Ocean for deep seabed mining, which is expected to commence in 2010.[4]

The Indian EEZ is extremely rich in fish stock. Although 3.9 million tons is estimated to be the annual sustainable yield, only 2.8 million tons is presently being exploited. Much of the catch (2.2 million tons) comes from coastal waters less than 100 metres deep since most fishing activity in India is by traditional means. Deep-sea fishing activity is negligible, considering that merely 160 deep-sea vessels are registered, many of which are not operational.[5] Employment of mechanised means for exploiting living resources of deeper waters and sea-bed, further out at sea, could provide an adequate source of proteins for the teeming millions of malnourished people and a solution to India's long-term food security.

The foregoing indicates that India's resource-harnessing perimeter in its maritime zone is gradually expanding outward. Of 'vital' interest to India, therefore, is the regulated behaviour of those using these waters adjoining the Indian landmass; what mariners call 'good order at sea'. The reasons could be economic, such as in terms of India's ownership of resources and security of offshore infrastructure and vessels involved in the economic activity; it could be environmental; and could even impinge on India's internal security. Of course, disorder at sea could also be result of the vagaries of nature, which leads to an 'important'[6] interest being the safety of human lives and property.

Island Territories

India's island territories comprising Andaman and Nicobar (A&N) archipelago in the east and Lakshadweep (Islands) in the west have long been perceived as among India's key vulnerabilities and even a security 'liability' due to their geographical distance from the mainland, particularly in case of A&N (See Map 4). Some of its islands had even demonstrated the propensity of 'slipping' away' from Indian control.[7] The perception of insecurity was further heightened by the fact that very few of these islands are inhabited; 36 of the 572 islands in A&N and 10 of the 36 islands in Lakshadweep.

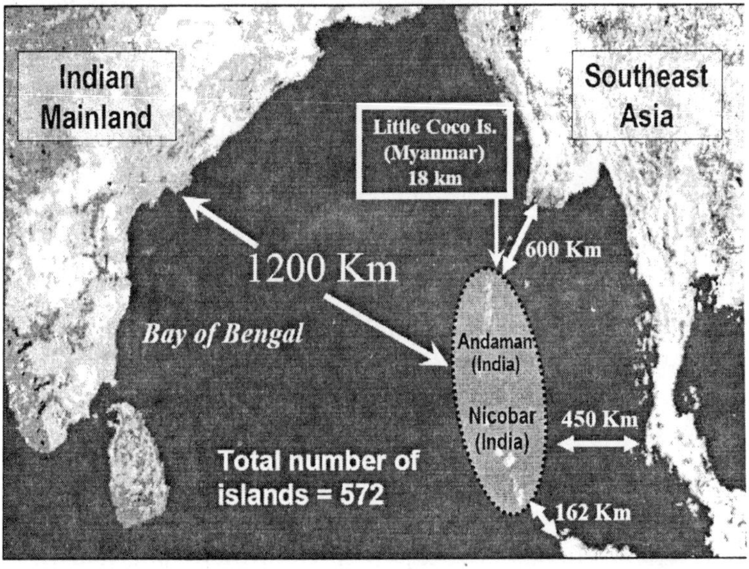

Source: Cdr GS Khurana

Map 4: India's Remote Andaman and Nicobar Islands

Lately, however, the significance of A&N and Lakshadweep is being increasingly realised. Located 1,200 km and 230-450 km respectively from the mainland, the two island chains expand both India's security perimeter and east-west reach of its maritime forces. Besides, these islands make four countries India's *maritime* neighbours – Maldives in the west; and Myanmar, Thailand and Indonesia in the east – which facilitates New Delhi's 'vital' linkages beyond its continental confines.

These islands bear tremendous economic potential as well. The A&N chain alone, though comprising only 0.2 per cent of India's total land area, contributes about 30 per cent to its EEZ. The hydrocarbon potential of this area has been mentioned earlier. The waters adjoining these coral islands also contain various species of untapped marine life that are highly prized as seafood and for a variety of other uses in the international market. VS Somvanshi, the Director-General of *Fishery Survey of India,* has indicated the high potential of developing economic activity here through export of seafood products to Singapore, which is located only 920 nm from Port Blair.[8] While A&N Islands are a vast storehouse of timber, coconut plantation in Lakshadweep has a huge industrial potential. Once sufficient infrastructure in these islands is developed with upgraded air and sea links, these could become attractive destinations for trade, investment and tourism. Some recent press reports have indicated that the process is underway, which is encouraging.[9] Some other writings even indicate plans to develop Port Blair as an international trade centre and for building an oil terminal and trans-shipment port in Campbell Bay (Great Nicobar Island) to cater to increasing maritime trade in the region.[10]

Overseas Trade

About 75 per cent of India's foreign trade in value and 95 per cent in volume moves by sea.[11] Such a high proportion of sea-borne trade is comparable to that of an island state, and this is due to India being geographically bottled-up within the sub-continent. Its landward communications beyond the subcontinent are severely restricted; not only owing to the natural topography (as mentioned earlier), but also due to political differences with Pakistan and Bangladesh. This makes the maritime outlet extremely critical for India's economic growth, particularly when the share of overseas trade in its GDP has been steadily increasing; from a mere 16 per cent in 1995, it rose to 28 per cent in 2005 and expected to reach 55 per cent by 2020.[12] Maritime routes are also vital for India's imports of energy resources (discussed later).

Another trend is the increase in eastbound trade flows. While the US and European states have traditionally been India's largest trading partners, India's trade with eastern Asia is increasing rapidly. An IBEF[13] report indicates that in 15 years since 1991, the growth of India's trade with its major trading partners in Southeast Asia and East Asia has ranged from four-fold to sixteen-fold. Quoting an IMF study, it adds that, "ASEAN+3 countries now account for the largest share of India's total trade at almost 26 per cent, followed by 24 per cent with the European Union, 18 per cent with the Middle East and 16 per cent with North America."[14] An April 2007 analysis of India's trade data indicates that 31 per cent of its merchandise trade currently moves east beyond the Southeast Asian straits.[15] This proportion may increase in the coming years with the regional Free Trade Areas (FTA) being established.

Strategic Imports

Commercial shipping is also important for imports of strategic resources, of which, fossil fuels are presently the most critical. India's growing thirst for energy resources is primarily due to its accelerated development. Presently, its commercial energy consumption is a *mere* 25 per cent of the world average – an apt indicator of the potential to be realised in coming years. Furthermore, coal remains a dominant commercial fuel in India, which is being replaced by natural gas. As the country's manufacturing sector develops further, imperatives of power generation would lead to an exponential increase in demand for gas. Despite new finds since 2002, India's own resources were inadequate to cater for its burgeoning needs. It began importing gas in 2004, and its import-dependence is expected to increase to almost 40 per cent by 2030.[16]

The demand for crude-oil resources is also rising rapidly due to the needs of public and freight transportation (sea, air and land) and the increasing number of private vehicles on Indian roads. During the past decade, India's oil consumption has grown by over 6 per cent annually, which is twice the world average growth.[17] While its annual demand was 40 million tons (mt) a decade ago, it is now 135 mt and is expected to increase to 370 mt in the next two decades.[18] However, the domestic production of oil has been stagnant and as per the *Associated Chambers of Commerce and Industry of India* (ASSOCHAM), India's current oil-import dependence of 70 per cent is likely to increase to 85 per cent by 2012.[19]

India's adversity in terms of barriers to its landward communications bears on its energy security rather severely. This answers some key questions – Why do the proposals mooted for overland gas pipelines to India often encounter 'rough seas'?

Why despite the geographic proximity to Central Asia, its ample natural gas reserves remain inaccessible to India? Why Bangladesh has denied India its surplus gas, and even a transit corridor for Myanmar's gas through its territory? It thus remains to be seen whether any of the proposed gas pipelines would ever reach India, but even if so, most of its natural gas imports would still continue to be sea-borne.

More than half of India's crude oil is presently sourced from the West Asian states like Saudi Arabia, Iran, Kuwait, Oman and the UAE. Some African states like Nigeria have also become India's major crude oil suppliers. India's long-term contract for liquefied natural gas (LNG) presently exists with Qatar, and such agreements are likely to be finalized soon with other countries like Algeria[20] . Indian companies also have also acquired energy stakes in West Asian states like Iran, Iraq, Syria, Sudan, Libya, Egypt and *Cote d'Ivoire.*

While India first turned to Africa to reduce heavy dependence on West Asia, it later made efforts towards source diversification to the East. Indian companies hold energy stakes in countries like Vietnam and Australia and Myanmar. Long-term contracts are currently being negotiated by India to import LNG from Malaysia[21] and Australia[22]. In Russia's Far East too, Indian companies have acquired substantial stakes since 2001. The first crude oil consignment of 90,000 tons from Sakhalin-I arrived in India (New Mangalore port) in early December.[23] Plans are also afoot for India to export its share of natural gas from Sakhalin-I as LNG.[24] The imperatives to diversify sources have also compelled India to look as far away as the Americas with Indian companies having acquired stakes in Cuba and Venezuela.[25] (Map 5 indicates the worldwide spread of India's energy sources, both current and potential). However, notwithstanding diversification

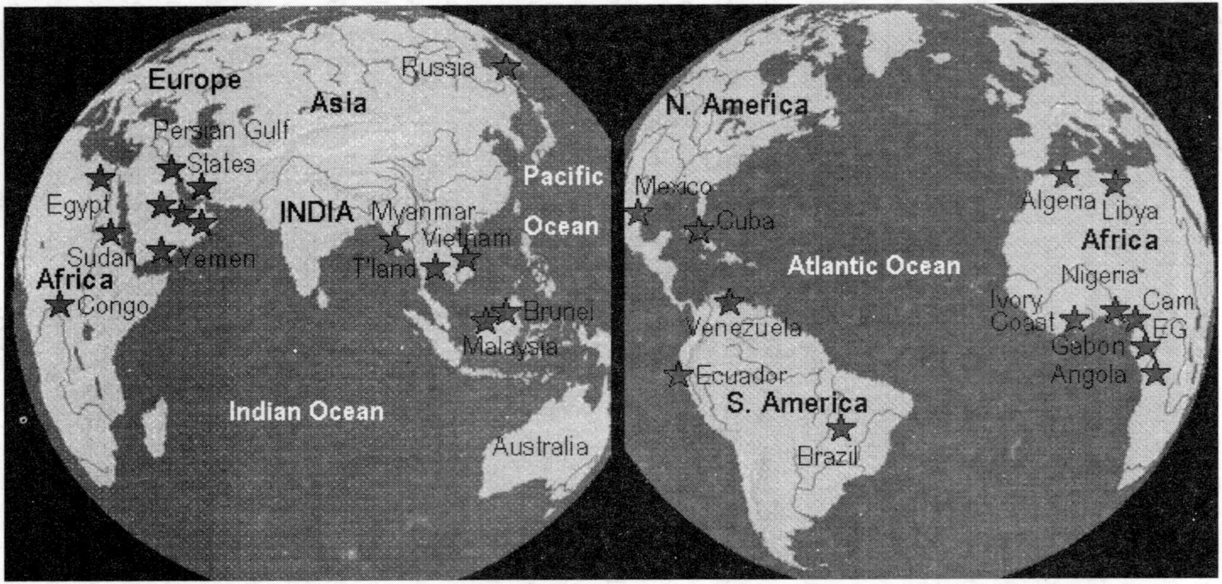

Source: Cdr GS Khurana

Map 5: Sources (and potential sources) of India's oil and LNG Imports

efforts, West Asia would continue to be India's principal energy source. This is premised on findings by an analyst that "while the (Persian) Gulf oil will last for 80 years, the non-Gulf oil will severely deplete in 15 years, unless production patterns change".[26]

As the Indian economy and the industrial output of its manufacturing sector develop further, Africa would also be a major source for other mineral resources such as nickel, cobalt, manganese and copper, which would assume greater salience as strategic commodities. Hence, India's vital economic stakes lie in stability of these regions and security of the sea-lines stretching from West Africa to Northeast Asia. Closer home, these interests also involve security of related infrastructure located in the littoral like ports, energy terminals and refineries.

Stability in the Indian Ocean Region (IOR)

The foregoing reveals that India's interests have expanded geographically beyond the Indian Ocean. However, the IOR remains intricately entwined with India's security. The entire gamut of its national interests, ranging from 'vital' interests like maritime communications to good order at sea to even 'survival' interests are underpinned by tranquillity in the Indian Ocean.

Closely linked to the desired 'benign' environment in these waters is the internal stability of the IOR littorals. However, the states represent the most diverse mosaic in the world in terms of most parameters, ranging from political systems to demographic size, and from per capita incomes to social development indices. Concomitant is the steadily growing potential for internal conflicts and centrifugal tendencies in countries that are at the lower end of this spectrum. Besides, their slow pace of economic growth and a weak technological base translates into inadequate investment towards security and law-enforcement capacity, something that does not augur well for the regional stability.

REFERENCES

1. Indian Maritime Doctrine, Integrated Headquarters, Ministry of Defence (Navy), April 25, 2004, p. 73.
2. 'Oil field auctions get 165 bids', *Times of India*, New Delhi, September 16, 2006, p. 17.
3. RR Choudhury, 'Energy Security Policy for India', IDSA *Strategic Analysis*, Vol XXI, February 1998, p. 1675.
4. Rahul Roy-Chaudhury. *India's Maritime Security*. IDSA and Knowledge World, New Delhi, June 2000, p. 50.
5. Dr. K Gopakumar, Former Deputy Director General (Fisheries), Indian Council of Agricultural Research, Seminar on 'Deep Sea Fishing in India', *National Maritime Foundation* (NMF), New Delhi, July 06, 2006.
6. Although the hierarchy of 'national interests' could be stated many ways, this paper classifies them into *survival, vital, important* and *other* interests.
7. In 1942, the Japanese captured them from the British without a fight. In March 1981, a Burmese naval gunboat landed troops on *Narkondum* Island. In 1985, a community of Thai fishermen were evicted from *Tillanchang* Island.
8. V.S. Somvanshi, 'Archipelagos within the Indian EEZ – Geographical Advantages and Opportunities for Fisheries Development', *Journal of Indian Ocean Studies,* 12 (2), August 2004, pp. 344-345.
9. Sourav Sanyal, 'Meanwhile, Port Blair for a Future with Phuket', *Indian Express,* July 25, 2005 at http://www.indianexpress.com/full_story.php?content_id=75059 (Accessed 17 Dec 05).
10. D. Sivaram, 'Geo-Strategic Implications of Sethusamudram', *Tamilnation* website, October 6, 2004 at http://www.tamilnation.org/forum/sivaram/041006.htm (Accessed 01 Nov 04).
11. Rahul Roy-Chaudhury, *India's Maritime Security*. IDSA and Knowledge World, New Delhi, June 2000, p. 1.

12. Premvir Das, Vice Admiral (Retd.), 'The Navy's Role in India's Emerging Security Concerns', *India Strategic*, Vol.1, February 2006, p. 50.
13. India Brand Equity foundation (IBEF) is a public-private partnership between Confederation of Indian Industry (CII) and Ministry of Commerce (Govt. of India).
14. 'India ASEAN: India's enduring commerce with rest of Asia', IBEF report, February 2005, pp.2-3 at www.ibef.org . Also see, Swati Lodh Kundu, "Asian surge in India trade", *Asia Times* online, May 28, 2005 at http://atimes.com/atimes/South_Asia/GE28Df01.html (Accessed 17 Dec 05).
15. 'India's Foreign Trade: 2007-08' (April), Division of International Trade, Department of Economic Analysis and Policy, RBI Monthly Bulletin, July 2007, p. 1279 and 1281, at http://rbidocs.rbi.org.in/rdocs/Bulletin/PDFs/78684.pdf (Accessed 01 Aug 07).
16. 'Findings of Recent IEA work 2005', OECD/IEA, 2005, p. 73. at http://www.iea.org/textbase/nppdf/free/2005/findings.pdf (Accessed 01 Nov 06).
17. Stein Tønnesson and Åshild Kolås, 'Energy Security in Asia: China, India, Oil and Peace', *International Peace Research Institute*, Oslo (PRIO) Report, April 2006, p. 40.
18. Ishrat Aziz, Ambassador (Retd.), 'Gulf Oil and India's Energy Needs', *India Strategic*, Vol.1, February 2006, pp. 48.
19. 'Crude Imports Requirement to Touch 85% By 2012: ASSOCHAM', *Associated Chambers of Commerce and Industry of India* press-release, August 16, 2007, at http://www.assocham.org/prels/shownews.php?id=1170 (Accessed 17 Aug 07).
20. 'GAIL to ink LNG deal with Algeria soon', *Times of India*, July 25, 2006, p. 10.
21. Based on information provided by Captain Mohedin Shahul Hameed, Senior Executive, Malaysia LNG Sdn Bhd, Petronas in September 2006. The process is still ongoing as per the available information.
22. Australia's LNG can however reach India only after 2011 since its order books are full till then. (As per discussions during the 5th Australia-India Security Roundtable, *Indian Council for World Affairs* (ICWA), New Delhi, 5-6 Dec 2006).

23. Sanjay Dutta, 'Sakhalin route to energy security', *Times of India*, New Delhi, December 8, 2006, p. 14.
24. 'India Plans to Liquefy Sakhalin Gas', *Reuters*, *The Moscow Times*, July 24, 2006 at http://www.themoscowtimes.com/stories/2006/07/24/049.html (Accessed 01 Aug 06).
25. Crude oil supplies from Venezuela have since begun to arrive in India. Parwini Zora and Daniel Woreck, 'India joins the scramble for oil', ICFI *World Socialist Website* (WSWS), April 12, 2005 at http://www.wsws.org/articles/2005/apr2005/ind1-a12.shtml (Accessed 01 Aug 05).
26. Ishrat Aziz, Ambassador (Retd.), 'Gulf Oil and India's Energy Needs', *India Strategic*, Vol.1, February 2006, pp. 48.

CHAPTER 3

Other Stakeholders in the Indian Ocean

As described in preceding chapter, India's security interests are inextricably linked to events in the Indian Ocean. However, it is also essential to factor the interests of the other 'stakeholders' in these waters – littoral states as well as extra-regional powers – to look for strategic 'overlaps', which form the underlying causes, either for cooperation or conflict. The following examines this aspect.

Regional Littorals

In varying degrees, the current trends in economic globalisation are leading to increasing stakes of regional countries in the Indian Ocean. Sea-lines are of 'vital' interest to all countries. The uninterrupted transportation of oil and gas is critical not only for the energy-deficient littorals in the region, but also for energy-exporting countries. For Gulf-states in particular, energy resources account for nearly all export earnings. This lead to their high stakes in the *Strait of Hormuz,* which is the only maritime exit of the Gulf and a transit route for approximately 88 percent of all petroleum oil exports of the Gulf-countries.[1]

The Indian Ocean littorals desire not only to preserve their sovereign rights over the respective maritime zones, but also to maximize the sea area under their jurisdictions (and thereby the share of maritime resources) by interpreting international law to their advantage. This is the underlying cause for India's unresolved maritime disputes with Pakistan and Bangladesh. Many states in Southeast Asia and West Asia also have such unresolved claims.

With their national policies focussed on economic development, regional countries desire to avoid armed conflicts and resolve disputes peacefully. However, owing to multifarious factors like uncertainties of the future, shape of geo-political environment, paucity of trust, political differences and the highly disparate capabilities, military insecurities persist in IOR. To secure their supreme national interests therefore, the littorals will be more inclined, either to acquiesce to power projection of major powers (in case of smaller and weaker states), or build sea-denial capabilities to deter them (in case of medium powers). Examples of the latter category are countries like Malaysia that are acquiring submarines, or Vietnam and Thailand which have plans to do the same. Even Bangladesh, despite its economic constraints, has expressed its intent to acquire such capability.[2] Pakistan is adding to its existing capabilities of submarines and adding more units armed with anti-ship missiles (discussed later).

A convergent interest among regional states is 'good order at sea', in terms of denial of sea; to those involved in unlawful acts like drug trafficking and smuggling of weapons that nourish non-state violence. This is of particular concern for states like Sri Lanka and Indonesia plagued by terrorism and centrifugal tendencies. It also applies to Australia, which is particularly wary of Islamic fundamentalists, who have often targeted its interests abroad. Like Malaysia and some other countries, Australia is also extremely anxious about illegal immigration. For Canberra, sanitising its maritime approaches of non-state threats thus becomes an important element of its 'maritime-citadel' approach to security. Management of disasters at sea is another common concern for security of commercial shipping and safety of lives at sea and in the littoral. An attendant interest is in preservation of the maritime environment.

The three littorals adjoining *Malacca Straits* (Malaysia, Indonesia and Singapore) present a unique case. With the waterway largely being their territorial waters (See Map 6), most of the littorals' maritime stakes – ranging from communications to exploitation of natural resources, and from internal security to even their 'survival' interests – are confined to this relatively constricted sea area. This, by itself, poses complex security issues for the Straits-littorals. The increasing global mercantile and military traffic transiting the Straits and the growing strategic significance of this waterway further aggravate the littorals' insecurity.

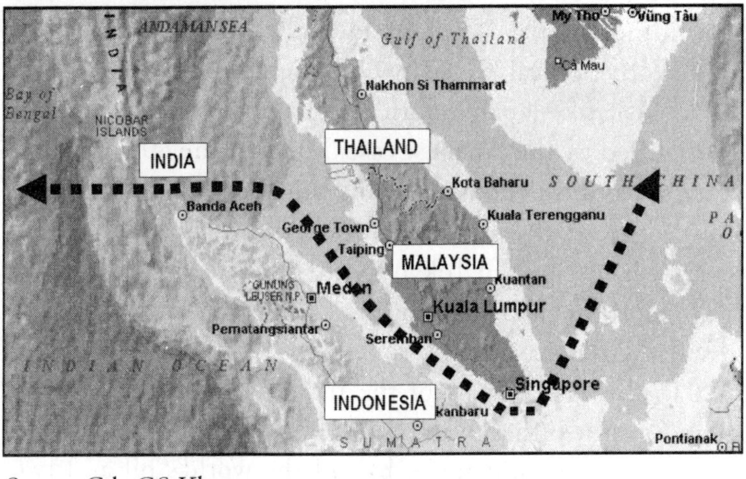

Source: Cdr GS Khurana

Map 6: Straits of Malacca & Singapore

Extra-regional Powers

As mentioned earlier, the Indian Ocean is geographically embayed by Asian landmass. This makes the Indian Ocean a relatively restricted passage for eastbound and westbound maritime communications, and thus, critical for sea-borne trade involving the extra-regional powers. With much crude oil and natural gas reserves located in Persian Gulf and Africa, the flows of these fossil-fuel resources across the Ocean are also increasing, and are mostly bound for industrial economies beyond the region. The *Strait of Hormuz* is of immense importance as a solitary maritime chokepoint of the Persian Gulf through which 17.4 million barrels of oil passes every day (as in 2005).[3] About 20 per cent of US oil imports are sourced from Persian Gulf.[4] Although Saudi Arabia's East-West 750-mile pipeline from Abqaiq to Yanbu (on Red Sea coast) provides an alternate route for oil supplies to the USA (and other western powers), the capacity of the pipeline is limited and thus, the *Hormuz Strait* continues to be of immense significance to the West. Besides, the maritime passage is particularly 'critical' for energy supplies to the American allies in East Asia like Japan, South Korea and Taiwan. This is best exemplified by the Japanese case. Much of the 80 per cent of Japan's crude oil demand transiting the Indian Ocean is sourced from the Persian Gulf. Compulsions of energy security have thus led Tokyo to extend its naval reach to this sub-region, notwithstanding the constraints imposed by its 'pacifist' Constitution.

In the eastern part of the Indian Ocean, the *Straits of Malacca* is the busiest waterway in the world though which, a quarter of the world trade, half of the world's oil and two-third of its LNG passing through it aboard nearly 70,000 vessels every year (See Map 6). It is therefore of immense importance to extra-regional stakeholders. It can be said that the *Malacca Straits* is more crucial than even the *Hormuz Strait* for the energy security of East Asian economies because the waterway provides transit to the oil and LNG sourced from Africa, in addition to the energy imports from Persian Gulf. These factors have lately become important drivers of China's policy making as well. 77 per cent of its oil crosses the Ocean and the highly vulnerable *Malacca Straits*. In order to mitigate its strategic vulnerability, China has been making intense efforts to build oil pipelines from various locations in the IOR like Pakistan (Gwadar)[5] and Myanmar (Sittwe/Kyaukphu)[6] and Malaysia (Yan)[7] to transport its strategic supplies to China (or the South China Sea). However, since this may be grossly insufficient, it is very likely that Beijing may plan for a 'physical' naval presence in the Indian Ocean.

Some extra-regional powers have continued to pursue a 'mercantilist' approach for access to natural resources across the globe and have therefore developed stakes in the IOR littoral. For example, China's state-owned companies have made substantial financial investments for offshore oil and gas exploration in countries like Kenya, Sudan (Red Sea), Iran (South Pars and north Pars), Bangladesh (Barakpuria), Myanmar (off Rakhine coast and in Gulf of Martaban), Sri Lanka (Puttalam-to-Hambantota coastal belt, Gulf of Mannar and Palk Strait). The need to secure these investments will reinforce the legitimacy of China's naval presence in these waters.

Besides for access to raw materials, the sea-lines crisscrossing Indian Ocean are also critical for extra-regional powers for market access for their exports, which are predominantly, manufactured goods.

These powers have other specific interests as well. For the US and its allies, military mobility and power projection across the Ocean has always been a vital interest to meet their *inter se* alliance commitments. The US has therefore continued to maintain its military bases and access agreements in IOR like Diego Garcia, Manama (Bahrain), Djibouti and Singapore. This has assumed even greater exigency after the terror strikes of September 11, 2001 on US territory. The US needs these facilities to counter threats 'at source' in West Asia and Southeast Asia, which have become the two fronts for the "war on terror". Even if some of these "bases" or "places" have to be wound up in the future, the US is likely to retain its presence though "sea-basing".[8] France administers two island territories in the Indian Ocean, namely Réunion and Mayotte, on the basis of which, it does not regard itself an *extra-regional* power, but belonging to IOR. Evidently, it desires to possess a capability to project power in these waters. This manifests in it being the only power besides the USA to maintain a separate Indian Ocean fleet and a major base in Djibouti, which is strategically located across the *Bab-el-Mandeb* choke point. As successor state of erstwhile Soviet Union, Russia's tangible interests in Indian Ocean have dwindled since the end of Cold War. However, it still maintains an occasional naval presence in these waters to have a continued sway in international relations.[9] The Russian strategic interest in these waters is likely to increase in the coming years. This interest is common to most other powers as well.

The Indian Ocean is also known to be a vast reservoir of seabed resources in the form of polymetallic nodules, which are known to contain manganese, iron, nickel, copper, cobalt and other minerals. As mentioned in the previous chapter, these resources have not yet been harnessed due to economic non-viability. In the future, as the development of seabed mining technology makes extraction of these resources easier and cost-effective, the salience of Indian Ocean will increase substantially.

REFERENCES

1. Rodrigue, Jean-Paul, 'Straits, Passages and Chokepoints: A Maritime Geostrategy of Petroleum Distribution', *Les Cashiers de Geographic du Quebec*, Vol.48, No. 135 (2004), p. 357.
2. Tim Shipman and Chad Bouchard, 'New arms race under the waves', *The Standard*, April 2, 2007 at http://www.thestandard.com.hk/news_detail.asp?pp_cat=20&art_id=41378&sid=12971022&con_type=1 (Accessed 04 Apr 07) and Nazrul Islam, 'Bangladesh to procure submarines…', *NewKerela*, May 22, 2006 at http://www.newkerala.com/news2.php?action=fullnews&id=63354 (Accessed 01 Jun 06).
3. World Energy Outlook 2005, OECD/IEA, 2005, p. 263.
4. The current oil consumption of the USA is about 26 million barrels per day (mbd), half of which is imported. PG contributes about 2.5 mbd.
5. Irfan Ghauri, 'Pakistan, China considering oil pipeline from Gwadar, *Daily Times* (Islamabad), May 24, 2006, at http://dailytimes.com.pk/default.asp?page=2006\05\24\story_24-5-2006_pg1_1 (Accessed 01 Aug 07).
6. Ian Storey, 'New Energy projects help China reduce its 'Malacca Dilemma', *Opinion Asia*, May 14, 2007, at http://www.opinionasia.org/NewEnergyProjectshelpChinareduceits Malacca Dilemma (Accessed 01 Aug 07).
7. ibid-, Also see, Prasun Sengupta, 'Looking East', *Force*, Vol.4 (9), May 2007, p. 24.
8. Though "Sea-basing", the US will maintain its rapid-reaction expeditionary capability including all dimensions of its military capability (land, sea, air and marines) based onboard aircraft carriers, amphibious ships like landing platform docks, other

warships like destroyers and frigates, submarines and also requisitioning commercial ships. The transition has already commenced.

9. Vijay Sakhuja, "Russian Navy's Surge into the Indian Ocean", *Asian Affairs*, July 2003 at http://www.asianaffairs.com/july2003/strategic_russian.htm (Accessed 01 Jul 05).

CHAPTER 4

India's Security Concerns

Military Conflicts

The Pakistan Factor

India does not envisage military threat from any of the regional littorals, except China and Pakistan. While an armed conflict with either one of these countries is not probable, it cannot be discounted in the foreseeable future. Notwithstanding India and Pakistan acquiring nuclear weapons capability in 1998, the possibility of a conventional clash between them has not ceased. Although Pakistan preferred 'sub-conventional' means to achieve its military objective in Jammu and Kashmir during the 1999 Kargil conflict, it could have led to full-scale hostilities if India had not displayed the restraint that it did in maintaining the sanctity of LoC (Line of Control). Notwithstanding the various confidence-building measures (CBM) instituted, such as prior notification of major military/naval exercises and the various *do's and don'ts* during these manoeuvres, India and Pakistan regularly snoop at each other's activities, which also bears a potential to spin out of control.

In case of an armed conflict, Pakistan will expect its naval forces not only to prevent recurrence of the reverses it encountered during the 1971 conflict, but also to adopt a more offensive posture to shape the outcome of war. Its maritime-capable force levels are currently undergoing a major qualitative and quantitative augmentation. The build-up is primarily focused at boosting sea-denial capabilities. Since 1999, Pakistan Navy has inducted three highly advanced French *Agousta*-90B submarines equipped with air independent propulsion (AIP), *Exocet* missiles and wire-guided torpedoes. Unconfirmed reports indicate the possibility of Pakistan acquiring three German U-214 submarines as well. These AIP boats are stated to be superior to the French *Scorpene* submarines being acquired by India, such as in terms of their stealth and greater maximum diving depth of 400 metres.[1]

With Chinese assistance, Pakistan has also been building missile-armed fast attack craft (FAC) indigenously, four of which have been added since late-1990s. The US sale of additional missile-armed F-16 and P-3C *Orion* aircraft will translate into a greater potency for maritime strikes. Lately, Pakistan Navy has also been laying significant stress on its anti-submarine warfare (ASW) forces in response to India's acquisition of the *Scorpenes*. Besides the *Orions*, induction of the Chinese Z-9C helicopters is aimed at boosting Pakistan's air-borne ASW capabilities. Its AIP submarines will also be effective submarine killers in defensive role. With the impending acquisitions of frigates from China (four F-22P) and Greece by 2012, the frigate numbers with India and Pakistan would be the same.[2] Pakistan is reported to have also approached Turkey in early-2007 for four corvettes.[3]

The China Factor

The Sino-Indian relationship continues to bear an adversarial potential, with the key contention being the border dispute. It is notable that while China has 'succeeded' in resolving its land-boundary disputes with all its neighbours, India and Bhutan continue to be the exceptions. The thorny issue of Tibet also cannot be ignored. According to Chinese records, Tibet was the "decisive factor" that led to the 1962 Sino-Indian conflict. Beijing's primary objective was to stymie Indian support to Tibet and thwart its attempts to convert it into a buffer zone (*huan chong guo*).[4] From the Chinese perspective, Tibet continues to be an irritant in relations owing to Indian government's permission to Dalai Lama to maintain quasi-governmental structures in India and the use of its territory by Tibetan exile community for anti-China activities. Beijing's worry is that India, in consort with the US, may try to restore Tibet as a buffer.[5] The continued existence of a strong Pakistan hostile to India is, therefore, of immense strategic value to China. This leads to the third major irritant in Sino-Indian relation – Chinese support to Pakistan aimed against India.

It is important to note that the aforesaid irritants have historical underpinnings, rather than being by-products of recent circumstances. China's antipathy to erstwhile colonial powers like Japan and Britain for its "century of humiliation" (*bainian guochi*)[6] is also directed against India, which China believes, has inherited British imperialism. From the Chinese viewpoint, India considers itself to be "natural successor of the great British empire," and wants Indian Ocean – the erstwhile 'British lake' – within its sphere of influence.[7] As regards the boundary issue as well, Beijing does not perceive it as post-decolonisation contention over a mere delineation of international border, but as its rightful claim to large territorial tracts under Indian "occupation", which it perceives, alike Taiwan, as being a legacy of the colonial era.

Among the various factors behind Sino-Indian political discord, the boundary issue bears the maximum potential for conflagrating into the use of military force, or the threat of its use. The possibility of a concurrent two-front war involving China and Pakistan also cannot be discounted.

India's insecurity could be particularly heightened when China establishes its naval presence in the Indian Ocean. With the enhancement of naval capabilities being among the predominant thrust of the Chinese military modernisation since the mid-1980s, its forays into the Ocean have already begun. This may be primarily driven by Beijing's concerns over the security of its jugular vein passing though the Ocean, which carries nearly 80 per cent of its oil imports sourced from West Asia and Africa. An article by PLA General Qian Guoliang (Commander of Shenyang Military Region) published in 2000 even linked this vulnerability to the "reunification" of Taiwan, which is currently China's foremost priority. Referring to the "crucial Chinese Communist Party (CCP) decision of 1999 on accelerating preparation for war", he wrote:

> "the threat perception is centred on the danger of 'one point' and 'one lane'." Here, the 'point' means "Taiwan's slide towards de jure independence", and the 'lane' refers to "the long voyage of China's oil tankers coming home from the Middle East and elsewhere (through the Indian Ocean)".[8]

This strongly reflects China's perception that its inability to 'control' Indian Ocean sea-lines poses a serious strategic constraint in terms of the Taiwan issue (or any future military conflict in the western Pacific). Given that the Chinese Navy is not expected to wield sea-control capabilities in the short-to-medium term, its submarines are more likely to be deployed. An analysis indicates that this is likely to happen latest by 2020-25.[9] This is reinforced by You Ji, a Chinese-origin expert on PLA Navy, who says that, "China's current strategy (in IOR) is ... to make its presence felt through building a credible naval strength. Submarines, at present, give China a short-run relief."[10] Other than deterring adversaries to interdict its strategic imports during hostilities, submarines' inherent attributes, like stealth, make them invaluable for other missions during peacetime (discussed later). Since nuclear-propelled submarines have nearly unlimited endurance, these boats are more likely to operate from the Chinese home bases. (The closest of these is the new underground submarine base 15 km east of Yulin naval base in south Hainan, which has been operational since 2006.) The conventional submarines will, however, need some basic facilities in the IOR to sustain their deployments for sufficiently long durations. Besides, all boats may also require technical support and supply of spare-parts in case of machinery/equipment breakdowns.

As mentioned earlier, the IOR littorals are either building naval capabilities due to their insecurities, or engaging the big powers to seek a favourable balance of power. This is likely to facilitate Chinese naval operations in the Indian Ocean. On its part, China has been making intense efforts to engage the IOR littorals through economic exchanges. It has been providing arms to countries like Myanmar, Bangladesh, Sri Lanka and Pakistan. Through financial and technical assistance, its is also assisting the littorals to build ports with maritime transportation infrastructure, such as wharves/ jetties, oil storage/bunkering facilities, etc. Examples of these are Gwadar (Pakistan), Hambantota (Sri Lanka), Sittwe (Myanmar) and Chittagong (Bangladesh). Since 2005, these 'nodes' of China's influence are being commonly being referred to as analysts worldwide as its "string of pearls" strategy[11] (see Map 7). Although these facilities

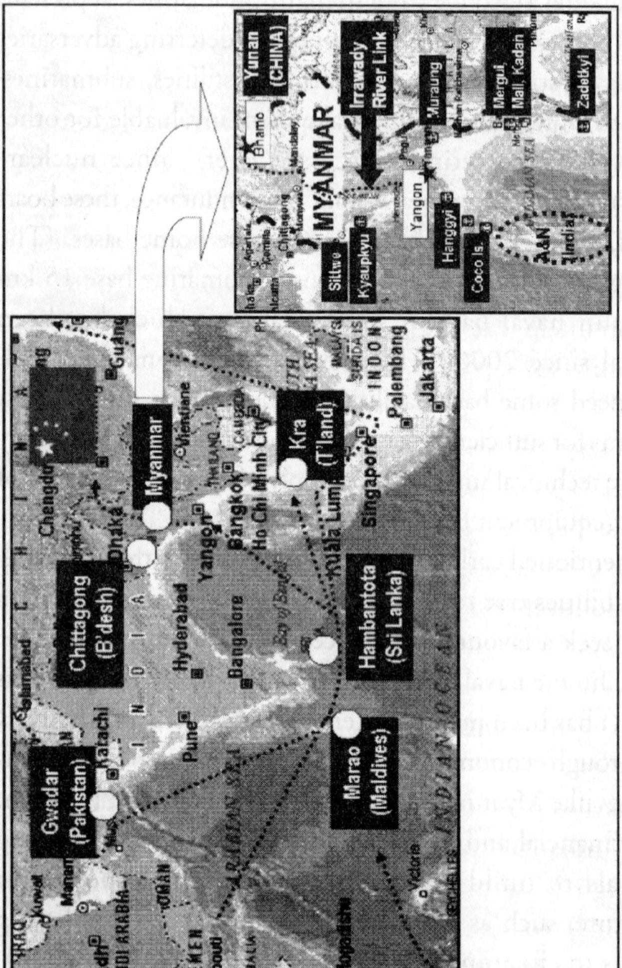

Source: Cdr GS Khurana

Map 7: Chinese "String of Pearls" in Indian Ocean

are ostensibly for civilian/commercial use, their 'dual-use' nature cannot be ignored – the facilities would be invaluable to sustain Chinese naval forces in the Indian Ocean. It is also important to note that since the early-1990s, China has been assisting Myanmar to build naval bases, airstrips, radars, electronic intelligence equipment and other military facilities in various locations along the entire Myanmar coast. China may seek access to these facilities or information since its technicians and instructors are known to be visiting these locations periodically, if not permanently manning these facilities. Unconfirmed reports also indicate the likelihood of Chinese-built electronic/communication intelligence posts in the vicinity of Gwadar.

Of all Chinese "pearls", Gwadar currently bears the maximum potential to impinge on India's security interests, particularly its energy imports from Persian Gulf. The use of Gwadar by PLA Navy will also be unpalatable for the US since this will enable Beijing to monitor activities of the US-led coalition in the Gulf. However, it is more likely that Islamabad will relent to political pressure from Beijing, considering the significant statement made by President Musharraf in 2004, "China has been our most consistent ally over the past 30 years...Washington's interest (in Pakistan) is likely to diminish."[12]

China has also planned for two transport corridors from China to the Indian Ocean. The road-rail-river (Irrawady) corridor through Myanmar connecting Kunming (China's Yunan province) to Yangon (Andaman Sea) is already operational. It cargo capacity is being augmented by more road-rail links and river dredging. Another is the project (being implemented) linking Kashi (China's Xinjiang province) to Gwadar (Arabian Sea) via a rail and road corridor through Pakistan. Although these corridors may have been primarily conceived to enhance economic connectivity, these could undeniably be used as logistics supply routes for Chinese naval forces operating in Indian Ocean, thereby substantially enhancing their staying power.

China's envisaged naval presence in the Indian Ocean severely complicates India's strategic calculus in the light of the prevailing paucity of trust and the relationship between the growing powers, where *competition* overbears *cooperation*. In case of a Sino-Indian military conflict, even China's minimal sea-denial capabilities in the Indian Ocean would severely complicate India's military-strategic calculus. Its attack submarines lurking off Indian ports could strangulate India's economy, and its submarine-launched land-attack cruise missiles (LACM) could be used to strike India's vital assets and installations in the littoral. Besides, its nuclear-tipped ballistic-missile submarines (SSBN) deployed in the Indian Ocean would make the Chinese nuclear threat *all-round* and indeterminate.

The PLA Navy is also pressing upon for addition of aircraft carriers in its doctrine. While refurbishment of the old Soviet carrier *Varyag* has begun in mid-2005, and concurrently, China is likely to be gaining expertise from it to build one domestically. With China's growing expertise for building large commercial vessels, its shipyards already possess the capacity to build a medium-sized carrier. Reportedly, China is also negotiating with Russia to purchase up to 50 carrier-capable Su-33 naval aircraft[13] and deck-landing systems.[14] Among other events, the commissioning of *Varyag* in PLA Navy as *Shilang* indicates a high probability of the Chinese navy operationalising a carrier in a decade or so. Carrier-borne aviation will be of immediate utility for Beijing to militarily assert its sovereignty claims in the South China Sea. Furthermore, once it develops an adequate power-projection capability based on carriers, China's military threat to India's island territories in the long-term timeframe is not inconceivable. It may be pertinent to recall that during World War II, Japanese forces had first occupied the A&N Islands with the intention of an assault on British India.

Military Confrontations Short of War

Maritime Boundary Disputes

While India's efforts to find peaceful solutions to its maritime boundary disputes with Pakistan and Bangladesh are underway, tensions persist in the disputed sea areas, and thus, so do the possibilities of localised skirmishes. Such incidents could be triggered by unilateral exploration or exploitation of resources in these waters. In 1981, a standoff occurred between India and Bangladesh over possession of *New Moore* Island, when Bangladeshi gunboats threatened an Indian survey vessel in the vicinity and an Indian corvette had to be sent in response.[15] The frequent harassment of fishermen in the waters in dispute with Pakistan is also a sensitive issue with a potential to flare up. Besides political and humanitarian issues, India's lingering contentions with Bangladesh and Pakistan bear the potential to adversely affect the states economically. In case the maritime boundaries are not resolved till 13 May 2009 (cut-off date for submitting claims for LCS), all three would lose sovereign economic rights over disputed areas to the international community.

Foreign Military Activity in Maritime Zone

Another security concern for India is the possibility of a military standoff involving an extra-regional naval power, for instance, if the latter conducts hydrographic or bathymetric surveys in

Indian waters, or any other military activity like live firing of weapons, launching of aircraft, and so on. In 2002-03 for example, the US naval research vessel USS *Bowditch* was noticed carrying out survey within Indian EEZ, and was asked by the Indian government to leave.[16] It is well known that UNCLOS is subject to varied interpretations with regard to foreign military activities in EEZ. The genesis of this legal 'void' can be traced back to the period when UNCLOS was being drawn up. Describing the negotiations, Rear Admiral OP Sharma says: "the maritime powers and developing countries (alike) somehow found it tactically advantageous to adopt a strategy of silence on military uses (of the seas) or security matters, both sides hoping to advance their interests by avoiding or minimizing controversy. Consequently, provisions of the Convention on these matters are ambiguous and allow ample room for difference of opinion".[17] The Law is based on the principal of *Mare Liberum* (Freedom of Seas),[18] but thus fails to answer the key question – When do national security considerations override claims based on navigational freedom? More specifically for example, while it states that "*Marine scientific research* in the exclusive economic zone and on the continental shelf shall be conducted with the consent of the coastal State",[19] it is silent on hydrographic survey. Such a survey can be justified as necessary for navigational safety, but which also has military applications, and thus bears the potential to severely impinge on the security of the coastal state (India in this case).

Many incidents of military showdown involving China have occurred in the western Pacific in recent years. Besides the aforesaid ambiguities in UNCLOS, Beijing's 'hard-line' approach has also contributed to these confrontations. While the USS *Bowditch* was also expelled by China from its EEZ, Chinese vessels have been conducting military activities and research in the maritime zones of other states without prior notification. In November 2004, Japan's Maritime Self Defence Force (JMSDF) units tracked a Chinese *Han*-class nuclear submarine in Japanese territorial waters. This could not be justified as 'innocent passage' under UNCLOS since the submarine's passage was *not in surfaced mode* (a legal requirement for innocent passage through foreign territorial waters). The Chinese government expressed "regret" for the incident, and stated it to have been caused by "technical reasons". This explanation, however, does not seem plausible since the vessel's track revealed that it had cruised submerged in "shallow waters for a number of hours", which also suggests the it was familiar with the underwater topography of the area.[20] Similarly, in November 2005, Japan's Coast Guard warned off a Chinese satellite tracking vessel from its *territorial waters* about 20 km south of the southern island prefecture of Okinawa.[21] The vessel 'technically' belonged to the Chinese Maritime Bureau, but it was reportedly manned by the PLA Navy.

In the event of Chinese naval presence in Indian Ocean, it can be assumed that its forces would be involved in hydrographic surveys, and possibly even intelligence-collection. Considering China's well-known propensity to use asymmetric means, it could also employ covert 'non-military' means for the purpose, such as scientific survey vessels in the guise of conducting energy exploration off Bangladesh and Sri Lanka, virtually adjoining the Indian territorial sea. China could also employ fishing boats for the purpose. In August 1994, the Indian Coast Guard captured three mysterious Chinese trawlers off *Narcondam* Island with charts showing hydrographic details of the area, one of which was equipped with electronic equipment. In October 2004, the trawler *Yu Man Shing* with a predominantly Chinese crew was seized off A&N Islands.[22] It is highly improbable that these Chinese fishermen had ventured 2000 nautical miles across the seas for illegal fishing. Hence, even if one were to discount the possibility of full-scale hostilities with China, its naval presence in the Indian Ocean bears immense potential for military discord.

Military 'Compellence'

The 'compellence' (commonly referred to as 'coercion')[23] of India by an extra-regional power using military force is also a possibility. As mentioned earlier, India was a victim of US 'gunboat-diplomacy' during the 1971 Indo-Pak War, when the USS *Enterprise* Carrier Battle Group (CBG) was deployed in Indian Ocean. According to Admiral SN Kohli (the Commander-in-Chief of Western Naval Command during the war, and later, the Chief of Naval Staff),

> "In Gunboat Diplomacy, the *biggest saving grace* (emphasis added) is when the interest of one power clashes with that of the other, which results in the simultaneous presence of the fleets of both powers in the area. For the smaller and weaker states, the *greatest danger* (emphasis added) occurs when only one power is left dominant in the area."[24]

In case of the US CBG deployment of 1971, while the US was the sole "dominant power" in Indian Ocean, and at that point of time, India fell in the category of "smaller and weaker states." The deployment of the countervailing Soviet power in the area would have been too late. The US move could not alter the outcome of war to India's detriment since the CBG reached Bay of Bengal only in the closing days of the conflict. It nonetheless did complicate India's strategic plans and distract Indian Navy from its main tasks.[25] This event thus became a major reason for India to build its naval power in the 1980s—to raise the cost of intervention by external powers.

Military Interventions/Instability in IOR

Although India's geographic centrality in Indian Ocean bestows upon it tremendous geo-strategic advantages, it could be at a major disadvantage as well. The big-power rivalry in the Ocean during Cold War was a source of immense insecurity. India's military assistance to Sri Lanka (1987-1990) and Maldives (1988) were also aimed at pre-empting intervention of the USA, which otherwise would have seriously undermined its security due to close geographical proximity and close ethnic linkages of these island states with India. The 1987 Indo-Sri Lankan accord specifically provided for *inter alia* removal of all foreign military and intelligence personnel from Sri Lanka and the commitment that neither Trincomalee, nor any other Sri Lankan port would be made available for military use by an external power.[26]

As discussed earlier, military forces of many extra-regional powers like the USA, France, UK and Russia have continued to operate in the Indian Ocean, with the USA and France also possessing island bases/territories. In the medium term, China, too, is likely to be able to project its military power across the IOR. Furthermore, considering its intensifying efforts to build 'nodes' of influence in the region, it is also not inconceivable for it to possess military bases in the IOR littoral states in the long-term timeframe.

As mentioned in Chapter 1, the smaller Indian Ocean littorals are highly prone to instabilities; due to their inadequate capacity for maintaining security and law-enforcement. Many of these states also have Indians working in significant numbers, who also send substantial amounts of remittances back home. The susceptibility of some African states to internal strife is growing as a combined effect of globalisation and the growing economic disparity within and among countries. Albeit not to the extent witnessed during the Cold War, these factors are certainly increasing the possibility of the powers intervening militarily. Notwithstanding New Delhi's current 'bonhomie' with the extra-regional powers, such interventions could be inimical to India's interests, particularly if these are carried out forcibly and are a result of strategic rivalry among the powers. The worsened security situation in Iraq after the US intervention is a case in point.

Security of Sea-lines/Strategic Imports

Military Threats

It is often said that in present times, military threats to sea-lines have receded in wake of economic globalisation and a common interest of countries in the safety and security of sea-borne trade. This follows a wider global phenomenon of reduced probability of major wars due to reduced focus on the issues of 'territoriality' in inter-state relations. However, the potential for armed conflicts in the Asian region cannot be discounted on account of exceptions like the Taiwan issue; and 'closer home', the Sino-Indian and Indo-Pak territorial disputes, which will invariably involve interdiction of strategic sea-borne imports. Besides, conflicts could also be triggered by the numerous contentions over maritime resources in the Indo-Pacific region, directly threatening commercial shipping. It is thus not surprising that states have continued to factor sea-line security in their military-strategic calculi, and much effort of strategic analysts is being devoted to reckoning the naval capabilities of potential adversaries as well as own vulnerabilities. On their part, the major powers have carried on the formulation of plans to control key maritime choke-points.

In case of India's military clash with a regional state, its imports of strategic resources would certainly be targeted by the adversary to degrade New Delhi's war-waging potential and break its will to continue with the war. The adversary would prefer to enforce a blockade of Indian ports (if it possesses adequate sea-control capabilities). If it is not capable of doing so, it will resort to *guerre de course* (literally, 'war on sea-lines') on India-bound vessels carrying strategic cargo. In case of a Sino-Indian conflict, it would be easier for China to interdict India-specific sea-lines close to the Indian ports, than it would be for India to attack Chinese shipping using international shipping routes of Indian Ocean due to the difficulty in sifting neutral shipping from the target. The use of facilities at Gwadar will be particularly helpful for the Chinese submarines to interdict the tankers carrying Gulf energy supplies to India's western ports. India may encounter insecurity off its eastern sea-board as well. To protect its energy investments off Myanmar coast, China is reported to have asked Pyinmana for greater "control" over its ports spread along the entire Myanmar coast facing the Bay of Bengal and Andaman Sea.[27] This translates into a potential threat to India's approaches to its Andaman and Nicobar Islands.

Even in case of a conflict not involving India, such as in Persian Gulf or western Pacific, Indian trade could be seriously threatened since the belligerents are likely to declare exclusion zones. A vessel carrying Indian cargo can also be attacked since, as mentioned earlier, discerning neutral shipping in the dense shipping of a sea-line is extremely difficult. During the Iran-

Iraq War in the Persian Gulf (1980-88), more than 500 merchant ships, including at least ten Indian-flagged vessels, became targets of sea-mines, aerial bombs, rockets or anti-ship missiles. The 'Tanker War' began with the two warring nations targeting each others' oil tankers to carry out the adversary's economic attrition. However, due to inaccuracy of shipping intelligence and targeting on both sides, it eventually turned into indiscriminate attacks on neutral shipping.[28]

Low-intensity Threats

The predominant insecurity to sea-lines today is posed by non-state actors. Sea piracy is the most prominent of these, which has been traditionally associated with the Southeast Asian waters. While the crime has been on the decline since its zenith in 2003, it now involves better planning, precise coordination and greater violence. While use of guns by pirates has increased sharply since 2001, heavier weapons like rocket launchers, grenades and machine guns have begun to be used since 2005.[29] Also, since 2005, the menace has become rampant off East Africa too, particularly off the coast of Somalia and in the Gulf of Aden.[30] In these waters too, the crime is associated with similar characteristics, leading to more casualties. In November 2005, a US-flagged cruise liner, *Sea-bourn Spirit*, was attacked using machine guns and rocket-propelled grenades,[31] leading a debate among analysts whether it was 'piracy' or 'terrorism'. (See photograph 1). In the coming years, such ambiguities are likely to manifest more often in Asian waters.

Map 8 depicts the piracy 'hot-spot' in the north-western Indian Ocean, which has since 2005, begun to rival an area of similar size in Southeast Asia traditionally infamous for pirate

Source: Wikimedia & MSNBC

Photograph 1: Case of MV *Sea-bourn Spirit*: The Victim-vessel, Pirates & Remnant of Rocket Attack

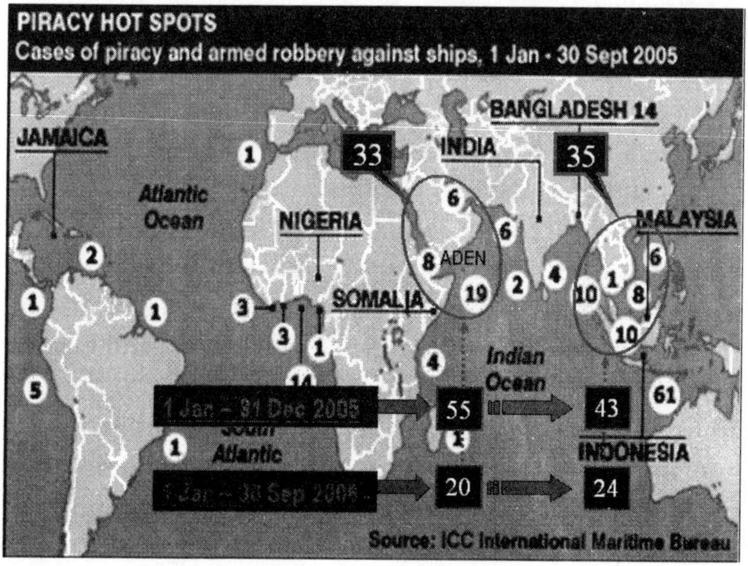

Source: Cdr GS Khurana

Map 8: Expanding Geographical Scope of 'Asian' Piracy since 2005

attacks. Piracy off the Nigerian coast is also on the rise, with the attacks primarily carried out against oil rig support vessels and tankers, thereby increasing the threat to the marine environment in the area.[32]

On many occasions, some insurgent groups such as *Free Aceh Movement* (GAM) in Indonesia and the *Liberation Tigers of Tamil Elam* (LTTE) in Sri Lanka have also resorted to piracy to further their political agenda. These separatists have often hijacked commercial ships in the past to loot cargo (in case of both GAM and LTTE), demand ransom (GAM), or use the captured vessels for illicit trafficking of drugs and arms (LTTE). While the threat from GAM has receded lately after its cease-fire with the government, it is also unlikely that the LTTE would carry out widespread attacks on global shipping since the group has a confined agenda. However, it may not be prudent to discount the threat completely. The well-known cases of the *Tamil Tigers* attacking commercial vessels are *Irish Mona* (1995), *Princess Wave* (1996), *Athena* (1997), *Misen* (1997), *Morong Bong* (1997), *Cordiality* (1997), *Princess Kash* (1988) and *M V Sik Yang* (1999). Since the 2006 renewal of LTTE-linked violence in Sri Lanka, the Tamil separatists have begun to target merchant ships again – vessels flying foreign flags off northern Sri Lanka, what they consider as "Eelam waters". In December 2006, the LTTE captured and burgled the Jordanian ship, MV *Farha-3* off Mullaitivu.[33] In January 2007, MV *City-of-Liverpool* was attacked off Jaffna while on a humanitarian mission.[34] The employment of bomb-laden suicide boats for the attack reiterates the 'hazy' dividing line between piracy and terrorism. The LTTE's tremendous potential to resort to 'high-intensity' violence against shipping is further evidenced by its frequent attacks on Sri Lankan naval craft, including those using *Scuba* divers. Given that the Sri

Lankan peace process has virtually failed and the LTTE-linked violence is likely to increase, the capabilities of *Sea Tigers* pose a serious threat to the shipping that will transit India's *Sethusamudram* canal.

The probability of terrorist attacks on energy transportation and infrastructure by Islamic radicals has also increased in the past few years, which leads to serious insecurities for India's energy resources sourced from Persian Gulf and Africa. While *Al Qaeda* is firmly entrenched in Weast Asia, reports indicate that Africa may become the next hotbed of the terrorist organisation.[35] Its nautical expertise to target stationary ships with fast boats packed with explosives was demonstrated with the *USS Cole* attack in Aden harbour in October 2000 (See photograph 2).

Source: http://fatvegan.com/2007/09/

Photograph 2: USS *Cole* after *Al Qaeda* attack in Aden Harbour

Using the same modus operandi, the slow-moving French supertanker *Limburg* was attacked off Aden in October 2002 (See Map 9). The attack was accompanied with Bin Laden's ominous warning to the West,

> "By God, the youths of God are preparing for you things that would fill your hearts with terror and

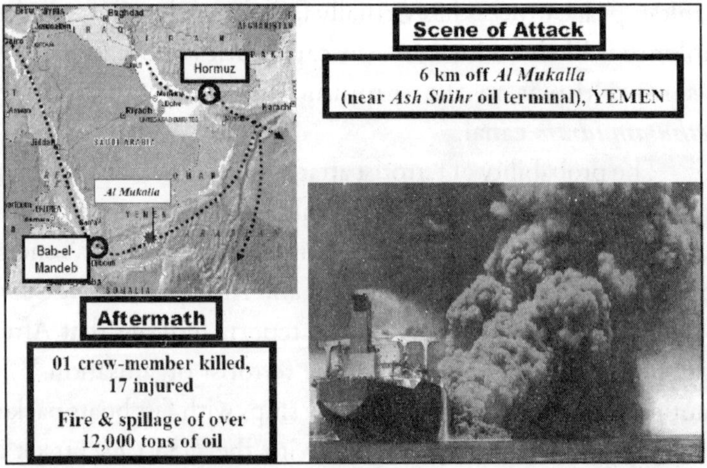

Source: The Jamestown Foundation

Map 9: Scene of *Al Qaeda* attack on MV *Limburg* (6 km off *Al Mukalla*, Yemen)

> target your economic lifeline until you stop your oppression and aggression."[36]

Soon thereafter, energy infrastructure became the primary targets of global terrorism, as indicated by events in the Persian Gulf, including the April 2004 *Al Qaeda* suicide attacks on Iraqi *Al Basra* and *Khor al Amaya* offshore oil terminals[37] (See Map 10).

Notwithstanding the presence of multinational naval forces, the Persian Gulf region continues to remain unstable. Besides instigation by *Al Qaeda*, the violence is closely linked to instability in Iraq, which is nowhere close to normalcy as yet. It is important to note that 90 per cent oil exports from Persian Gulf are sea-borne[38] and Bin Laden has specifically expressed his 'penchant' for "...oil facilities in the Persian Gulf...the main artery of the Americaneconomy".[39] This implies a persisting terrorist threat to

Source: Michael Yon & http://www.someoneelseslife.com/?m=200603

Map 10: Iraqi Oil Terminals attacked by *Al Qaeda* in April 2004

the Gulf's offshore platforms, loading berths and oil/LNG tankers; besides the risk to shipping transiting through the choke points like the *Strait of Hormuz* and *Bab-el-Mandeb*. Fears are often expressed that terrorists could scuttle a huge hijacked vessel in these choke points, thus blocking the route for other ships with grave consequences for global economy, including spiking insurance rates. These are, however, unfounded since the navigational channel in these straits is at least 3 km wide, and their minimum depths are 30 metres and 80 metres respectively (See Map 11). Nonetheless, in case the terrorists could lay crude sea-mines, an activation of even one by any vessel would be sufficient to disrupt energy exports for many days due to the fear among the shippers.[40]

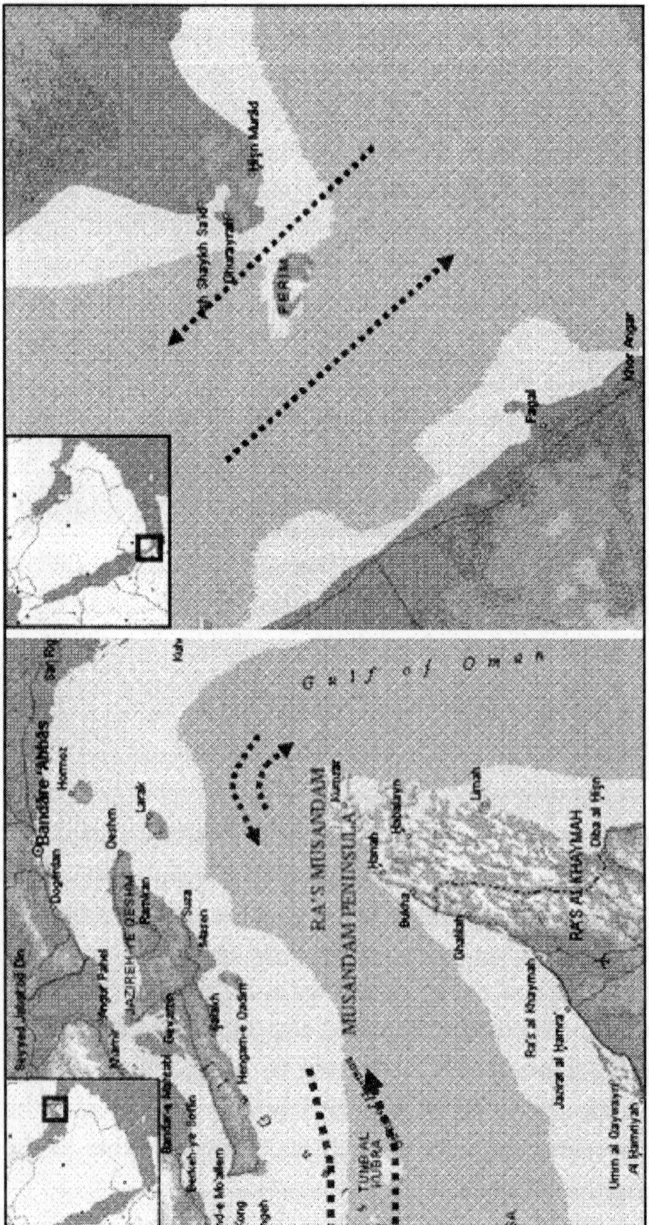

Source: Cdr GS Khurana

Map 11: *Strait of Hormuz* (left) & *Bab-el-Mandeb* passage (right)

In the eastern Indian Ocean, the sea-lines passing through straits of archipelagic Southeast Asia are highly insecure as well. Essentially, this is due to the 'insecurity-triad' in the region formed by maritime crimes (like piracy, drug trafficking and weapons smuggling), separatist movements and Islamic fundamentalism. The rampant crime in these waters stems from the 'maritime traditions' of its people that resurfaced in the late-1990s in the form of unlawful acts at sea. The anxieties are not unfounded – the three elements of the triad could forge symbiotic bonds. For example, it is well known that the Islamic radical group *Jammah Islamiyah* (*Al Qaeda* offshoot) has been beckoning separatists in Indonesia, the Philippines and southern Thailand with *jehadi* calls.

By virtue of its global criticality (and more so for the US and its allies), *Malacca Straits* is the most threatened. There have been no attacks by terrorists in the waterway so far, probably since their 'nautical skills' are not yet developed. But it is widely believed that it would be feasible for them to use the expertise of the pirates to carry out attacks on shipping. There is no concrete evidence yet of such a nexus, or that the intensity of 'threat' is increasing. However, the 'risk' to shipping activity is certainly on the rise due to the growing 'vulnerabilities' of the Straits.[41] The mercantile traffic through the waterway is increasing, adding to local activity like inter-island ferries and fishing. The tonnage of ships is also growing, thereby reducing their ability to manouver due to severe navigational constraints. The challenge is posed by the relatively less channel width, and particularly, the shallowness of waterway, lined with dangerous shoals and shipwrecks (Map 12 below depicts the extent of navigational constraint posed to a very-large crude-carrier of *Malaccamax* size – the largest vessel permitted to transit the *Malacca Straits*).

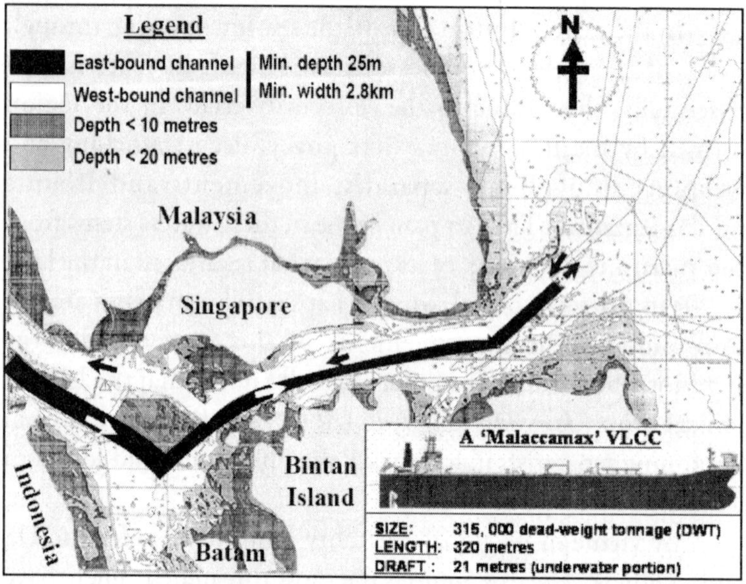

Source: IEA (http://www.iea.org/textbase/speech/2004/ramsay/seoul.pdf)

Map 12: *Straits of Malacca*: A Challenge for Navigation

These constraints compel ships to cruise at slow speeds, making them vulnerable to being boarded by pirates, and which also imperil their navigational safety. Also notable is the increasing proportion of vessels carrying inflammable liquids like crude oil and LNG, and other dangerous cargo like ammonium nitrate. As per an International Energy Agency (IEA) report, oil traffic through the *Malacca Straits* is expected to double to 22 million barrels per day by 2030.[42] Besides increasing its vulnerability to maritime violence, this will make the Straits more susceptible to accidents involving collisions and groundings, which may also lead to marine pollution through oil-spills. Attendant to the increasing sea-borne trade is the growing capacity of ports to handle cargo, making these 'worthy' targets for terrorism. Some major hub-ports of the world like

Singapore and Tanjung Pelepas are also located along the waterway. The vulnerabilities of the Straits are accentuated by those of the shipping industry, particularly in terms of the vessels flying *Flags of Convenience* (FoC),[43] which are characterised by low safety standards and lax manning regulations.

As depicted in Map 12, the navigable channel of the *Malacca Straits* is only 25 m deep at the shallowest, and 2.8 km wide at the narrowest. Thus, as in case of *Hormuz Strait* and *Bab-el-Mandeb*, it may not be practically possible for terrorists to block the passage by capsizing a large vessel. However, in June 2006, the Malaysian defence chief said, "the terrorists could plant sea-mines, which could be as crude as explosives packed in oil-drums, or even sophisticated ones, incorporating trigger-devices."[44] Through this, he not only indicated not only the possibility of the disruption of trade through mining, but also their growing ability of the terrorists to use novel methods of attack, ranging from 'high-asymmetry' to 'high-end technology'. Besides, a major attack on a hub-port in the Straits using a vessel carrying dangerous cargo would create sufficient psychological reverberations to effectively and severely disrupt global trade.

The aforesaid indicates an increased risk to shipping activity (even if not the threat *per se*), both in terms of its geographical scope and tenor. Given India's expanding stakes, this translates into a heightening of the insecurity to Indian shipping (including those carrying energy resources), which traverses through these areas, or will do so shortly. Besides, it is important to note that most countries/ regions from where India's energy resources are sourced or where India has acquired energy stakes (Sudan, Nigeria, Syria, etc.) are plagued by geo-political and ethnic instabilities. It may also be pertinent that many of the oil and gas fields in these countries are located offshore.

Maritime 'Disorder' at Sea

The 'disorder' at sea mainly manifests in form of unlawful activities in the maritime realm by a variety of non-state actors ranging from terrorists and criminal syndicates to ordinary people in search of livelihood from the oceans. (To facilitate better understanding, 'piracy' as a crime impinging on sea-line security has been examined separately and thus not included in this section). The disorder also involves the peril to human lives at sea due to natural causes or human errors.

Terrorist Strikes in Maritime Zones

Security threats to India's maritime economic zones have not yet materialized, but are being increasingly acknowledged. While economic assets (offshore) also present themselves as military targets, the current threat is primarily from anti-national elements or terrorists, which may act either independently or in consort with foreign state agencies. These concerns were also expressed by India's Home Minister Mr. Shivraj Patil in end-2006. Addressing top police officials in New Delhi, he said, "Some *Lashkar-e-Toiba* operatives are being trained specifically for sabotage of oil installations".[45] Besides the offshore energy installations, at high risk are the vessels involved in economic activity or scientific survey.

The risk is actually growing with time. As noted in Chapter 2, India's offshore resources are presently sourced from Bombay High relatively close to the western coast and the various river basins virtually adjoining the eastern coast. In the coming years however, when the hydrocarbon reserves are tapped from off the far-flung islands and the LCS, the extraction rigs will be located further away from the coast, thus increasing their assailability to both state and non-state threats in direct proportion to the distance.

Besides, considering the relatively lesser distances presently involved today, the extracted oil and gas are transported to refineries/ consumers ashore via submarine pipelines, the longest being 200 km. Such pipelines are evidently more secure relative to tankers. In the future, as the distance of the extraction sites from the Indian mainland increases, these resources (and products) will need to be transported over large transit distances. India may then need to rely more on tankers, since the submarine pipelines would not be cost effective. This would raise India's vulnerability further.

Contraband Smuggling

A substantial proportion of criminal activity involving illegal transfers of narcotics and weapons/explosives in India's neighbourhood uses sea transportation, predominantly in its eastern waters, but also off its western seaboard (See Map 13). The drug trade criss-crosses southern Asia from the '*Golden Crescent*' in its west (Pakistan, Iran and Afghanistan) and the '*Golden Triangle*' in its east (Myanmar, Thailand and Laos). Funds raised from the sale are used to purchase small arms, explosives and even sophisticated weaponry in countries like Afghanistan and Cambodia, where plenty of these are available at low prices, left over from conflicts in the past. The port of Ranong in Thailand is known to be the hub of a clandestine arms market. From here, weapons are smuggled by well-networked criminal groups to their affiliates in other parts of the world using FoC ships (many of these owned by LTTE), whose ownership and movements are difficult to track.[46]

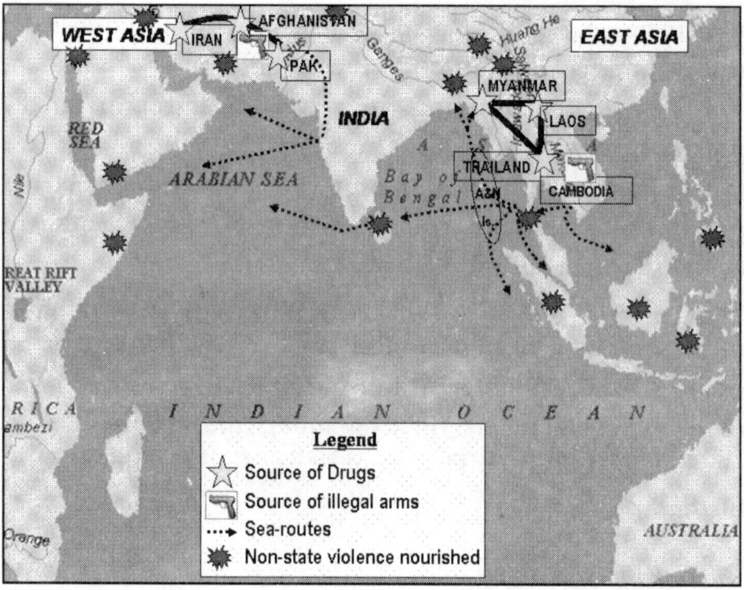

Source: Cdr GS Khurana

Map 13: Sea-routes used for Drug Trafficking and Gunrunning in IOR

These organised crimes impinge on India's internal security since it provides nourishment to insurgent violence and terrorism. India's extensive and porous coastline could be easily exploited by covert activities of states or anti-national elements. It is well known that explosives used during the 1993 Mumbai serial blasts had been transported via the Arabian Sea. While terrorism in Kashmir is mostly nourished across land border, the insurgents operating in India's north-eastern states are known to obtain their arms and explosives via fishing boats across Andaman Sea, landed either on to the coasts of Myanmar or Bangladesh, from where Indian militants receive supplies through land routes. In 1997, the Royal Thai Navy intercepted arms off Ranong meant for insurgents in Manipur. Bangladesh has seized fishing vessels in the process of dumping arms on its coast on many occasions. The revelations of various operations *Leech* and *Poorab*[47] conducted off A&N Islands in 1998 also confirmed these connections. Due to the close proximity, maritime security off these Islands is closely linked to that in the archipelagic waters and straits of Southeast Asia and primarily the security of *Malacca Straits.*

Proliferation of Weapons of Mass Destruction

While the amorphous threat of terrorism can be extrapolated by 9/11, it constitutes only the 'visible horizon' of the extent of the terrorists' innovation. They are likely to be on the lookout for new means to cause mass effect, which may even include transfer of weapons of mass destruction (WMD)[48] to their intended target. As part of the vulnerable global trading system, commercial ships are widely acknowledged to be the most suitable vectors. Although the security of airlines has been beefed up, worldwide since 9/11, maritime transportation remains a 'weak link' due to the inherently unregulated nature of the ocean realm and assured freedom of navigation at sea. The ease of concealment within a ship and the growing containerisation of trade have compounded the problem of such illicit transfers.

India is not removed from this insecurity, since there is sufficient evidence of the growing 'jehadi' links of the terrorists groups operating in India's (provincial) state of Jammu and Kashmir with the global terrorist network of *Al Qaeda*. In any case, the country is at high risk since it lies midway in the 'arc of *jehadi* terror' automated spanning West Asia to Southeast Asia.

To counter the WMD threat that may seek ingress through its ports, India has neither a mechanism nor the capacity for sanitising the shipping traffic, both in their seaward approaches, or within the ports. In October 2004, ten workers at a private foundry near Delhi were killed by a blast caused by live shells in the metal scrap imported from erstwhile war zones of West Asia in shipping containers.[49] In May 2005, a large quantity of small arms was discovered at Mumbai port in a shipping container that had arrived from Singapore.[50] More recently in March 2007, a similar cargo was revealed in a Karachi-bound ship docked at Kochi.[51] Fortunately, none of these ships were carrying WMDs, but these amply expose India's vulnerabilities. The terrorists' access to WMDs in a similar way cannot thus be discounted, particularly considering that it is feasible to inspect only 2 to 3 per cent of the containers manually after being offloaded, and most Indian ports do not yet possess the technology for 'non-intrusive' (automated) inspections.

The Vulnerable Island Territories

The probability of a state posing a direct military threat to India's A&N Islands is low. However, as mentioned earlier, owing to the unpredictability of the regional security scenario beyond the medium term and the inherent vulnerabilities of the island chain, it may not be prudent to discount the threat totally.

India's island possessions are particularly vulnerable to low-intensity threats. In February 2007, the Indian Naval Chief warned that some uninhabited islands could become terror-hubs and "launch pads" (staging areas) for terrorists trying to infiltrate to the Indian mainland.[52] The far-flung, widely scattered, and mostly uninhabited, A&N Islands are located close to Southeast Asian states infested with insurgencies and Islamic terrorism and are thus prone to clandestine activities of these groups. It was also revealed during the operations *Leech* and *Poorab* conducted in 1998 (mentioned earlier) that these islands have also been used as transit halts for gunrunners and drug traffickers using small fishing boats to ferry contraband across Andaman Sea.

Lakshadweep also bears the potential for criminal activity and instability. Only ten of its thirty-odd islands are inhabited, wherein 96 per cent of the population is Muslim. While there has been no past incidence of violence in these islands, the influence of Islamic fundamentalists sponsored by the Pakistani Inter Services Intelligence (ISI) cannot be ruled out in the future. The strategic location of this island chain also makes these suitable as transit halts by Islamic terrorists smuggling arms and drugs across the Indian Ocean.[53]

The A&N Islands have been attracting foreigners, particularly those from the neighbouring Southeast Asian littorals, to engage in illegal fishing and poach other marine organisms in its waters. The 'fetch' from these waters, which abound in varied species of seafood and other marine organisms, is sold back home at very high prices. The easy availability of hi-tech nautical equipment in these countries like radar, refrigeration plants and global positioning system (GPS) miniaturised for small boats, facilitates evasion, endurance and precise navigation. This could have been checked to an extent if the local fishing industry was developed with the fishermen seeking deep-sea catches and not confining themselves to traditional non-mechanised means of fishing. It is also important to bear in mind that 'illegal fishing' in Indian waters by foreign fishermen can have grave security implications for India, much beyond depletion of fish stock and ecological imbalance.

The same holds good for illegal immigration (or human trafficking), which also bears a potential for serious longer-term security implications since it could lead to social unrest. It is known that many people from Myanmar, Bangladesh and Sri

Lanka (Tamils) have settled down in A&N Islands. The demographic characteristics of these islands make it easy for these 'outsiders' to merge with the local populace and eventually leads to socio-economic tensions, criminal activity and polarisation of society along communal lines. The possibility also exists of the Chinese intelligence or ISI elements infiltrating these groups for information-gathering and subversive activities. This poses a daunting challenge for Indian security forces because if such transfers are not interdicted at sea, it would become extremely difficult to take corrective measures later when humanitarian considerations become overriding.

'Reverberations' of Instability in Sri Lanka

Undoubtedly, the LTTE agenda (of creating Eelam) is confined to the Sri Lankan territory (and territorial waters), and its leadership wants to keep it so. However, the instability in the island-state poses grave security challenges for India due to geographical proximity and ethnic links between the two peoples. A variety of threat scenarios emanate from the current situation in Sri Lanka, which manifest (or have the potential to do so), both in and across the maritime space separating the two states, viz. Gulf of Mannar, Palk Bay/Strait and the adjoining waters.

The foremost threat is posed by the significant capabilities of the LTTE's naval wing (*Sea Tigers*), which has virtually made it the 'third navy' in the area. This reality is pregnant with future dangers for India, including the threat to *Sethusamudram* canal. Even at present, the increasing clashes between *Sea Tigers* and Sri Lanka Navy in these waters has led to an increasing insecurity for fishermen, who recognise no maritime boundaries, and depending upon the endurance of their boats, go wherever the fish can be caught. The growing casualties among Indian fishermen due to frequent incidents of firing by Sri Lanka Navy[54] reiterate the risk to their lives due to the difficulty of positive identification. (One must, however, concede the possibility of LTTE involvement in the firing, it is not yet clear).

The instability in the island-state may have been triggered by the repression of Tamil minority in the 1970s. It has, however, aggravated to the present level due to the substantial material (besides monetary and ideological) support that the LTTE have received from a large Tamil Diaspora abroad, including a significant populace in Tamil Nadu.[55] This is amply indicated by the seizure of fishing boats in the interposing waters, carrying explosives and other terrorist-related material from Tamil Nadu to northern Sri Lanka.[56]

The influx of Tamils into India, to escape the turmoil in Sri Lanka, is another cause for insecurity. Although this can be checked by Indian maritime forces, this is unfeasible due to humanitarian considerations. The issue becomes even more complex since it is highly possible for the *Tamil Tiger* guerrillas to infiltrate into Tamil Nadu in the guise of refugees to regroup and plan their operations. In case the violence in Sri Lanka escalates, there could be an exodus of refugees into Tamil Nadu, with attendant strain on resources of state and national infrastructure.

Maritime Accidents/Disasters

Another disorder at sea is through natural disasters at sea and shipping accidents like collisions and groundings. The Bay of Bengal is particularly susceptible to nature's fury with cyclones here being as frequent as two to four per year, each time causing much devastation deep inland of India's eastern coast and at sea.

The Indian Ocean *Tsunami* of December 2004 indicated that the worse is indeed possible. The littorals of the northern Indian Ocean were caught unawares and were unprepared for a disaster of this magnitude in terms of an early warning mechanism and its management. Few Indians were aware of the existence of an active volcano in their country until Barren Island (Andaman) erupted in 1991. It has since erupted on many occasions subsequently, the latest being as recently as in May 2006. The natural phenomena reminded India that the earth's crust under its maritime east is highly prone to turbulence.

Linked to these disasters is the threat to the marine environment. Notwithstanding the implementation of various global measures in this direction, including stringent regulations for oil tankers, major oil-spills have continued. As a result of the growing energy requirements of the regional states, the numbers and size of tankers crossing Indian maritime zones is increasing rapidly, and as a consequence, the potential for oil-spills in these waters. This seriously threatens marine eco-systems, with severe long-term ill effects on fish stocks. The sea area around India's A&N Islands is particularly fragile in this regard and thus very susceptible to such imbalance. These ill-effects of marine pollution are already discernable in waters off South Nicobar Island, which lies adjacent to the congested international shipping traffic of the six-degree channel. This is likely to spread northwards – as noted in Chapter 3, China intends building an oil pipeline from Myanmar to its Yunaan province to avoid transporting its strategic imports through the vulnerable *Malacca Straits*. Chinese tankers moving across Bay of Bengal to discharge their cargo at Sittwe/Kyaukphu may lead to a similar effect in Indian EEZ off the Andaman Islands.

REFERENCES

1. Tariq Iqbal, 'Pakistan may acquire three U-214 submarines from Germany', *Pakistan Defence*, April 23, 2007, at http://www.defence.pk/news/publish/Pakistan_may_acquire_three_U-214_submarines_from_Germany_20070423.php (Accessed 13 Aug 07).
2. Shiv Aroor, 'After China, Pakistan turns to Greece to build its frigate fleet', *Indian Express*, May 17, 2006, at http://www.indianexpress.com/printerFriendly/4594.html (Accessed 04 Apr 07).
3. Turkish Press, 25 February 2007, at http://www.turkishpress.com/news.asp?id=164229 (Accessed 04 Apr 07).
4. Chinese history of 1962 war published by China's Academy of Military Sciences (AMS) and other authoritative sources, cited in John W. Graver, *Protracted Contest: Sino-Indian Rivalry in the 20th Century*, University of Washington press: Seattle/ London (2001), pp. 59-60.
5. ibid., p. 78.
6. Period between mid-19th and mid-20th centuries, when foreign powers subjugated China and caused immense sufferings to its people. Peter Hayo Gries, *China's New Nationalism* (California/London: California University Press, 2004), pp. 43-53.
7. Michael Pillsbury, 'China's Strategic Outlook', in K Santhanam and S Kondapalli (ed.) *Asian Security and China 2000-2010* (New Delhi: IDSA and Shipra Publications, 2004), p. 99 and 105.
8. General Qian Guoliang, "Quanmian luoshi 'silinbu jianshe gangyao', gaobiaozhun zhuahao silingbu jiguan jianshe" (comprehensively implement guideline of headquarters construction, and do a good job at headquarters construction), *Journal of the PLA National Defence University*, no. 6, 2000, p.4, quoted by Dr. You Ji (Univ. of New South Wales), Paper presented at the National Maritime Foundation (NMF) seminar on 'China & IOR' at New Delhi on 13-14 Oct 06.
9. This is based on a classified study undertaken by the author.
10. See, Conference Report, IDSA-PRIO International Conference

on 'The Geopolitics of Energy Security: The Rise of Asia', New Delhi, 15-16 December 2006, at 15-16 December 2006, at http://www.prio.no/files/manual-import/CONFERENCE%20REPORT%20GEOPOL.pdf (Accessed 05 Aug 07).

11. The phrase "String of Pearls" was first used in a 2005 report by Booz-Allen-Hamilton, "Energy Futures in Asia" prepared for US Defense Secretary. 'String of Pearls Military Plan to protect China's oil: US Report', Space War, January 18, 2005 at http://www.spacewar.com/2005/050118111727.edxbwxn8.html (Accessed 05 Jul 07).
12. Zahid Hussain and Jay Solomon, "Pakistan's Ties to Beijing Face New Challenges; Abduction of China Workers Forces Musharraf to Balance Militant War, Ally Interests," *Wall Street Journal,* A.20, October 12, 2004, cited in Ammad Hassan, 'Pakistan's Gwadar Port: Prospects of Economic Revival', *Naval Post-graduate School Monterey (California),* June 2005, p. 45.
13. 'China to Buy Su-33 Fighter from Russia', *SinoDefence.com* new-report, October 24, 2006 at http://www.sinodefence.com/news/2006/news06-10-24.asp (Accessed 12 December 06).
14. 'Chinese Navy to build two carriers with Russian help – agency', *RIA Novosti,* (Russian News & Information Agency), July 27, 2007, at http://en.rian.ru/world/20070727/69828953.html (Accessed 05 Aug 07).
15. Rahul Roy-Chaudhury. *India's Maritime Security.* IDSA and Knowledge World, New Delhi, June 2000, p. 65.
16. 'US ship spied in Indian waters', *The Acorn,* June 05, 2004 at http://acorn.nationalinterest.in/?p=578 (Accessed 10 Dec 04)
17. The Admiral represented India at the UNCLOS-3 deliberations. For details, see Rear Admiral (Retd.) OP Sharma, 'Ocean Governance: Potential Areas of Conflict' in *Securing the Oceans: An Indian Ocean Perspective,* National Maritime Foundation (NMF), New Delhi, Seminar Proceedings, Jun 04, 2005, p. 53.
18. Literally, 'Free Sea'. A theory propounded by the Dutch jurist Hugo Grotius in 1609 AD, which contradicted the theory of *Mare Clausum* (Closed Sea) advocating that the ocean space, like land territory, could be claimed and controlled by nations.
19. UNCLOS, Part XIII (Article 246).

20. East Asian Strategic Review (2005), *National Institute for Defense Studies* (NIDS), Japan, p. 105 & 120.
21. 'Japan Warns Off Chinese Navy Vessel in Japanese Waters', *Reuters* (Tokyo), *Defence News*, November 11, 2005 at http://www.defensenews.com/story.php?F=1248227&C=asiapac (Accessed 17 Dec 05).
22. VK Shashikumar, "Beware of the Dragon", *Tehelka*, New Delhi, December 18, 2004, p. 5.
23. In military parlance, however, 'Compellence' is different from 'Coercion'. While the latter is a compulsion posed on the adversary to abandon his *military* objective by the threat of destruction of his assets, the former is an act short of war, where there is a *political* objective to change state behaviour by the threat of destruction caused by war. See, Indian Maritime Doctrine, pp. 22-23.
24. Admiral (Retd.) SN Kohli, PVSM, AVSM, 'Relevance of the navy in nuclear age', *Indian Express*, July 28, 1978. Quoted by same the author in *We Dared. Maritime Operations in the 1971 Indo-Pak War*. Lancer, New Delhi, 1989, p. 123.
25. Rahul Roy-Chaudhury. *Sea power and Indian Security*. Bressey's, London & Washington, 1995, pp. 74-77.
26. ibid., p. 137.
27. Prasun Sengupta, 'Looking East' *Force*, Vol.4(9), May 2007, p. 24.
28. Sreedhar and Kapil Kaul. *Tanker War*. ABC Publishing House, New Delhi, 1989, p. 1, 4 and 87.
29. Sam Bateman, CZ Raymond and Joshua Ho, 'Safety and Security in the Malacca and Singapore Straits: An Agenda for Action", *IDSS* Policy Paper, May 2006, p. 25.
30. 'Piracy on the rise off Somalia', *BBC News*, November 8, 2005 at http://news.bbc.co.uk/2/hi/africa/4415196.stm (Accessed 17 Dec 05).
31. Statement issued by *Securewest International* on 7 November 2005, cited by *Cargo Security International* website http://www.cargosecurityinternational.com/channeldetail.asp?cid=9&caid=5865 November 7, 2005 (Accessed 31 October 06).
32. 'Marine piracy spikes in second quarter of 2007: watchdog', *IC Publications* website, July 12, 2007, at http://www.africasia.com/

services/news/newsitem.php?area=africa&item=070712091150.zavpq57i.php (Accessed 05 Aug 07).

33. The items burgled were radar, computers and communication sets. The Jordanian authorities confirmed charge of piracy against LTTE. Walter Jayawardhana, 'Jordan confirms Tamil Tigers pirated ship', *Asian Tribune*, December 24, 2006 at http://www.asiantribune.com/index.php?q=node/3826 (Accessed 01 Mar 07).
34. 'Sri Lanka military catches LTTE in another act of piracy', *Sri Lankan Daily*, January 21, 2007, at http://www.colombopage.com/archive_07/January21140512CH.html (Accessed 25 Jan 07).
35. 'Is Africa next Qaida haven?', *Times of India*, September 1, 2006, p. 23.
36. "Station Airs Alleged Osama Tape", *CBS News*, October 6, 2002 at http://www.cbsnews.com/stories/2002/09/13/attack/main522015.shtml (Accessed 07 Aug 05).
37. "Suicide Boat Bombers Attack Key Iraqi Oil Terminal", *Jihad Watch*, April 24, 2004 at http://www.jihadwatch.org/archives/001704.php (Accessed 17 Dec 05).
38. *EIA* Fact Sheet, September 2004 at http://www.eia.doe.gov/emeu/cabs/pgulf.html (Accessed 17 Dec 05).
39. "Map of Future Al-Qaeda Operations", *SITE Institute*, February 14, 2005 at http://www.siteinstitute.org/bin/articles.cgi?ID=publications19805&Category=publications&Subcategory=0 (Accessed 17 Dec 05).
40. Cdr Gurpreet S Khurana, 'Maritime Terror off Arabian Peninsula: A Post-*Limburg* Security Assessment', *West Asia in Turmoil: Implications for Global Security*, NS Sisodia & Ashok K. Behuria (ed.), IDSA & Academic Foundation, New Delhi, 2007, p. 95.
41. 'Risk' is essentially a function of 'threat' and 'vulnerability' and directly proportional to these factors.
42. William C. Ramsay (Deputy Executive Director, IEA, Paris), "Asian Oil: Current Trends, Outlook and Issues', Presentation to Conference on '*Regional Cooperation: Key to Energy Security*', New Delhi, January 6, 2005, at http://www.iea.org/dbtw-wpd/Textbase/speech/2005/ramsay/asianoil.pdf (Accessed 08 Mar 06).
43. Today, many ship-owners prefer to register their vessels in countries like Panama, Honduras and Liberia for easy registration with low

or non-existent taxes and no restrictions on safety standards or crew nationality.

44. 'Malaysian Military Warns Underwater Mines Could be Terrorist Tool', *Agence France-Presse* (Kuala Lumpur), *Defence News*, July 6, 2006 at http://www.defensenews.com/story.php?F= 1853798&C= navwar (Accessed 01 Dec 06).
45. Sudha Ramachandran, 'India moves to secure its shores', *Asia Times* online, December 22, 2006, at http://www.atimes.com/atimes/South_Asia/HL22Df01.html (Accessed 04 Apr 07).
46. By FoC registration, the ship-owner not only saves on money and efforts to meet standards, he can hide his identity from official scrutiny, enabling his vessel to operate incognito. With such vessels frequently re-named, re-painted and re-registered, it compounds the difficulty to track them.
47. These were anti-gunrunning operations conducted jointly by the Indian armed forces and intelligence agencies in February and May 1998 respectively. 'Myanmar offered arms for lending a helping hand' *Hindustan Times*, September 12, 1998 at http://www.ibiblio.org/obl/reg.burma/archives/199809/msg00419.html (Accessed 4 Apr 07).
48. The term "WMD" is normally understood to comprise nuclear (including radiological), chemical and biological weapons.
49. Jyotsna Singh, "Perils of India's scrap metal", *BBC* online, October 13, 2004 at http://news.bbc.co.uk/1/hi/world/south_asia/3739512.stm (Accessed- 16 Feb 05).
50. 'Major arms haul at Mumbai port', *Tribune* News Service, May 21, 2005 at http://www.tribuneindia.com/2005/20050522/main3.htm (Accessed 4 Apr 2007).
51. 'Kochi arms haul tip of iceberg: Navy chief', *Hindustan Times*, March 8, 2007, at http://147.208.132.198/news/181_1947196,0008.htm (Accessed 4 Apr 2007).
52. 'Uninhabited islands could become terror hubs: navy chief', *The Hindu*, February 23, 2007 at http://www.hindu.com/thehindu/holnus/001200702232172.htm (Accessed 4 Apr 2007).
53. Vishwas Varghese, "Yet another Kashmir in the making?", September 18, 1999 at http://www.swordoftruth.com/

swordoftruth/archives/byauthor/vishwasvarghese/yakitm.html (Accessed 1 Jun 05).

54. Jaya Menon, 'DMK to protest in front of Lanka mission', *Indian Express,* New Delhi, March 11, 2007, p. 10.
55. A provincial state in South India adjacent to Sri Lanka. Its capital is Chennai.
56. 'Tamil Nadu and LTTE menace", *The Hindu*, February 22, 2007, at http://www.hindu.com/2007/02/22/stories/2007022201081000.htm (Accessed 04 Apr 07).

CHAPTER 5

India's Policy Imperatives

It may have become amply clear from the preceding chapters that India's *primary* area of strategic interest is the Indian Ocean. Undeniably, however, its vital interests are steadily expanding beyond this region. For example, India's increasing trade and energy flows east of the Southeast Asian straits and the need to deter and achieve leverage against potential adversaries in Asia have stretched the eastwards limit of its strategic frontiers. Similarly, with its energy imports being increasingly sourced from West Africa and Latin America, the westward extent of its area of interest has also dilated. However, India's present articulation[1] limits the area of India's strategic interest to within the IOR due to non-availability of commensurate capabilities, primarily in terms of its ability to maintain naval presence beyond the Indian Ocean.

The Three Broad Imperatives

The imperatives for India to meet its security challenges, within and beyond its stated strategic frontiers, are mainly three-fold. The foremost is the capacity-building of Indian maritime forces to meet their increasing responsibilities. One could consider the other two imperatives together as *building security bonds with other countries*. However, this needs to be divided into two parts, viz. security cooperation with the *regional littorals* and that with the *extra-regional powers*. While the two components may even be coincident in some case, segregation is necessary for the sake of clarity in comprehension, besides some fundamental differences between the two.

The contours of the three broad imperatives are examined below. It is important to note that these are not exhaustive – a state needs to apply all the resources at its disposal to achieve its grand-strategic/national security objectives, including through support to its maritime forces (as examined in Chapter 4, the Chinese case is exemplary in this context). Hence, New Delhi will also need to resort to politico-diplomatic and economic engagement of key states, promote defence exports to the IOR littorals, and even project soft power overseas. However, accounting for these is beyond the scope of this writing.

Capabilities of Maritime Forces

While building capabilities, the foremost emphasis must be on maritime domain awareness (MDA), a critical necessity for all maritime forces. The two essential requisites for achieving it are ISR (Intelligence, Surveillance and Reconnaissance) and C^4 (Command, Control, Communications and Computers). MDA essentially is a summation of maritime information needed to build a common surface and air picture at a central command node, and dissemination of the picture and its analysis in real-time down the command chain to operational units, which will also need to be linked laterally. The inputs will need to be obtained from numerous sources – ranging from satellite-based, air-borne, ship-based or coastal sensors to the data collected during warship deployments and intelligence analyses. As in case of ISR, such real-time networked data transfer will need a high level of technology, towards which, the Indian Navy has devoted much effort, particularly through implementation of projects like NEWN (Navy Enterprise Wide Network).[2]

Given India's expanding strategic stakes and the spatial proliferation of regional threats, the capabilities of Indian Navy will need to be tailored in terms of greater reach and sustenance. A 'long-legged' blue-water navy needs to be configured in the medium term to enable power-projection and sustained military operations, at least up to the farthest points of India's *primary* area of strategic interest. Although this will require a high capital investment, the comprehensive picture and current realities are being increasingly realized in India. Significant strides have been taken by the Indian policy makers in this direction, but some critical voids are yet to be addressed. The need to have 'longer-legs' however does not in any way indicate that the significance of Navy's *constabulary role* is diminished; it has actually gained greater relevance, but this role would now have to be discharged at larger distance from the shores.

The responsibilities of Coast Guard are also expanding with India's increasing reliance on the seas for natural resources, which is necessary to sustain its economic growth and development. The force needs to have sufficient assets and law-enforcement capacity to enable it to respond to the full spectrum of low-intensity threats in the entire maritime space under India's jurisdiction – not only the current 200 nm EEZ, but also in the space that will enclose the future LCS. However, this relatively young service, with only about 60 ships and 45 aircraft presently, operates with severe constraints. This is why many naval assets are tied down with brown-water tasks. The *Perspective Plan – 2002-2017* was envisaged to correct this anomaly through increasing the force-level to 169 ships and 99 aircraft, but it is realized that even this may not be adequate.[3] The Coast Guard would need to be supplemented by marine police of coastal states. (These imperatives are examined in detail later). The implementation of appropriate policy decisions with regard to marine police and Coast Guard would provide the Navy with greater 'leeway' to pursue its primary responsibilities.

However, no state can secure its interests with its own resources alone, which is particularly true for the maritime realm, whose inherent attributes make its complete regulation virtually impossible even for the most potent of the naval powers. A pointer to this is the latest US concept of "Thousand-ship Navy", which envisages securing the American overseas interests through a partnership of the navies of "like-minded" nations.[4] Furthermore, given the increasing trans-national character of current threats, it becomes necessary to view security issues within a region holistically in a 'systemic' sense. This brings forth the other two imperatives, viz. engagement/ maritime security cooperation with both the regional littorals and extra-regional powers. As examined later in detail, such bonds are also necessary to further the state's foreign policy.

Regional Security Cooperation

The inclusion of India in ASEAN Regional Forum (ARF) in 1996 was a manifestation of New Delhi's successful efforts at engaging the Southeast Asian nations since the launch of its Look-East policy in early-1990s. Although this policy was largely driven by economic incentives, it is lesser known that barely a year after the formal India-ASEAN contact was established; India invited the Southeast Asian states for a joint naval exercise in Oct 1992, which took them by surprise.[5] India evidently wanted to lose no time in forging security bonds with the sub-region.

With the exception of ARF, a multilateral security arrangement has always been difficult to achieve in the region due to the vastly divergent threat perceptions among states. Even ARF has not been able to achieve any substantial success in issues of maritime security. The *Indian Ocean Rim Association for Regional Cooperation* (IORARC) was a 'non-starter' in terms of forging security bonds. Security cooperation within *South Asia Association for Regional Cooperation* (SAARC) has not yet gone beyond joint-declarations. While deliberations on counter-terrorism in SAARC meets have not yet yielded any meaningful results, maritime security issues have not even been discussed. Although some suggestions have been made for a security mechanism among littorals of *Bay of Bengal Initiative for Multi-Sectoral Technical and Economic Cooperation* (BIMSTEC), this has not yet been actively considered, probably due to India's political differences with Bangladesh.

India has taken the initiative to create a new multilateral security arrangement through the Indian Ocean Naval Symposium (IONS). If IONS succeeds, it could not only address many of India's prevailing insecurities, but also serve as a platform wherein the resources of the more-capable regional powers could complement the security/law-enforcement capacities of the smaller states. To sustain IONS however, the more powerful states including India would need to resist the temptation to dominate centre-stage. Also, 'hard' security issues and purely military/naval approach to these will need to be avoided, at least until adequate trust among the regional countries is developed.

Notwithstanding IONS, India's focus on bilateral approach to forge security bonds should not be abandoned. Given that India's geographic location makes its role crucial in regional security, mobilising political will of regional countries has not been difficult. Many of these countries have had close naval interactions or maritime security ties with India since long – these include Singapore and Vietnam in Southeast Asia; African littorals like Kenya and Mozambique, and the Indian Ocean island-states: Maldives, Mauritius, Seychelles and Sri Lanka. These ties are being reinforced, as is exemplified by the following:

- The increasing complexity of Indo-Singapore naval exercises (called SIMBEX),
- The July 2007 Indo-Vietnam defence agreement, wherein maritime security figured as a major component.[6]
- Maritime surveillance for countries like Mauritius and Mozambique (since 2003), and
- Assistance to Maldives in conducting hydrographic surveys.

In addition to strengthening the existing bonds, Indian maritime forces have begun forging new bonds with their counterparts in other littoral countries, within IOR and beyond. India's growing security ties with Myanmar are very evident from the increased reciprocal warship port calls and high-level military visits since 2002 (details later). For New Delhi, this is essential not only to mitigate Beijing's influence in Pyinmana, but also for maritime security in the northern Bay of Bengal. In April 2007, Indonesia formally acceded to a security and defence agreement with India to cooperate, *inter alia*, on training, maritime-boundary patrols, terrorism and sea-piracy.[7] In June 2007, India and the Philippines conducted joint coast guard exercises in Manila Bay.[8] Indo-Japan cooperation has also accelerated since the first contact between their coast guards in the year 2000 (covered in the next sub-section). Even Australia, whose primary focus has traditionally been on the Pacific Ocean, is increasingly realising that its security interests converge with those of India. In June 2006, its Defence Minister backed India's "policing of the Indian Ocean" and stated that the two countries had "agreed to develop maritime cooperation and exchanges that enhance mutual capacity"[9] The Indian Navy has also intensified efforts to engage the Persian Gulf states. In August 2007, two flotillas of Indian Navy undertook a 20-day long deployment to the Gulf, making port calls in nearly all sub-regional states – Kuwait, Saudi Arabia, Qatar, Bahrain, Oman and the United Arab Emirates (UAE) – and conducting joint naval exercises after each port visit. This has been India's largest ever naval interaction with the Gulf littorals so far.[10] Events are thus in the process of validating the opinion of some analysts, who had indicated the interest of Persian Gulf states in "a wider participation in Gulf security arrangements to include countries like China and India".[11]

The most pressing requirement is to engage immediate maritime neighbours to counter trans-national threats across maritime boundaries. However, serious impediments exist for forging security bonds with neighbours like Pakistan and Bangladesh due to outstanding maritime/ political disputes. The way forward would require confidence-building measures (CBM). These have a good chance of succeeding since maritime issues have been least contentious in the otherwise 'prickly' relationship with the two neighbours. These could accrue much benefit to both sides in terms of relief for the fishermen and prevention of incidents at sea. Indo-Pak concord is also necessary for their continental shelf claims, and the same holds good for Bangladesh. India's offer for hydrographic assistance to the two countries towards compiling the necessary data in connection with its claim would be a positive symbolic gesture.

Given that the Sri Lankan peace process has virtually failed and the LTTE-linked violence is likely to increase, the cardinal question is whether Sri Lankan Navy has sufficient wherewithal and blunt the capability of *Tamil Tigers*. This is unlikely considering that even Indian Navy could not succeed in severing the LTTE's overseas supply routes in nearly three years of Operation *Pawan* (including the preparatory phase preceding the deployment of Indian military forces in Sri Lanka in 1987). It is hardly surprising therefore that Sri Lanka is seeking Indian assistance to achieve this. The Indian policy towards Sri Lanka requires to be thoughtfully worked out because New Delhi is clearly caught in a conundrum: while it is necessary to prevent human rights violations by Sri Lankan government forces on Sri Lankan Tamils, the *Tamil Tigers* must be 'tamed' to catalyze the peace process. To make matters more complex, India does not wish to intervene militarily once again. This has led of India's apparent indifference to the issue, which, very 'dangerously', amounts to a vacation of a key 'strategic space' and works out to India's detriment in the longer term. India has been involved in capacity-building of Sri Lanka Navy through assistance in training and providing offshore patrol vessels (OPV),[12] but more proactive measures by its maritime forces may be required to choke LTTE's military logistics to weaken its capabilities (This issue is examined later in greater detail). Of course, this will need to follow an understanding with Colombo on the human rights issue.

Cooperation with Extra-Regional Powers

The presence of external naval powers in Indian Ocean continues today, even after the end of Cold War. During those years, India was among those countries that opposed such naval presence most vociferously. However, the changed politico-security paradigm today has made it advantageous for India to strive for cooperation with these powers, for which it needs to explore the convergence of interests. This imperative assumes greater salience considering that it may not be realistic, at least in the medium-term timeframe, for Indian Navy to seek the capacity to project military power beyond the Indian Ocean.

The increasing global commitments of the US maritime forces and the attendant 'overstretch' of its limited resources are obvious. Coupled to India's increasing regional eminence (in terms of both its geographic location and growing comprehensive power), this is leading the US to seek India's cooperation to safeguard its own maritime security interests in the IOR. During the US operations in Afghanistan in 2002 (Operation *Enduring Freedom*), its request to India for naval escort of its high-value ships through *Malacca Straits*[13] can be seen in this context. The rationale of other powers like France, Russia and the UK to forge security ties with India is also strongly driven by their interests in IOR. This quest manifests, *inter alia*, in the increasing frequency of India's structured exercises with their navies like *Malabar* (USA), *Varuna* (France), and *Indra* (Russia). The Indo-US Maritime Cooperation Framework of March 2006 even indicates, albeit implicitly, that the US desires India's participation in coalition operations.[14] Although Indian Navy cannot be expected to act as an 'appendage' of any big-power navy, given the contemporary global scenario, there may be areas of common interest and complementarities, which may make it necessary for India to undertake joint-operations with US forces. More explicitly, the US has been seeking an institutionalized long-term agreement for access of its naval units to Indian ports.[15] Reports indicate that India may soon accede to this "logistics support agreement" on a reciprocal basis.[16] In the coming years, it may be necessary for India to enter into similar agreements with other extra-regional powers as well.

The quadrilateral (Australia, India, Japan and the USA) effort in response to the Indian Ocean *Tsunami*, of end-2004, was one scenario where India and Australia worked with the extra-regional powers to fulfil their normative obligation towards regional tranquillity and at the same time meet their common interests. Securing sea-lines against non-state actors, preventing their access to WMDs and maintenance of regional stability are scenarios that are more likely to involve convergent stakes and necessitate joint responses, including those mandated by the UN.

India and Japan have taken significant strides in enhancing maritime security cooperation since the April 2005 visit of the Japanese Prime Minister to India. The joint statement following the visit had merely emphasized upon the importance of 'maritime security' and 'instructed' Indian Navy and JMSDF 'to enhance their cooperation'.[17] In contrast, the joint statement following the visit of Indian Prime Minister to Japan in December 2006 was a 'concrete' step forward. It 'urge(d) their concerned (defence) agencies to develop an annual calendar of cooperation and exchanges' and even set a timeline for joint naval exercises.[18] The first of these was conducted in 2007.[19] It is also evident that as the Indian economy grows, the strategic congruence between New Delhi and Tokyo is likely to strengthen because of two factors; *first*, the growing Asian economic integration, and *second*, the geographic locations of India and Japan *vis-'a-vis* the global distribution of potential sources of strategic commodities.[20] Although sea-line security is the principal driver of increasing cooperative ties between maritime forces of India and Japan, many avenues for joint operations may emerge as the Japanese government takes incremental steps to free its maritime forces from the constraints posed by provisions of the Japanese Constitution. The upgradation of Japanese Defence Agency into a Ministry[21] may be considered as a precursor to this evolution.

Security cooperation with extra-regional powers will however necessitate 'operational compatibility' among the forces. The increasing frequency, rigour and scope of India's joint naval exercises with major powers aim to achieve this. Further, given that such 'operational compatibility' needs to be achieved at both procedural and technological levels, the need for a high-level of equipment sophistication, performance and interoperability would bring dividends for India in terms of 'self-audit' of own defence preparedness, exposure to new operational concepts and training value, and access to advanced military hardware and technology to bridge its capability-voids.

It is also necessary to engage China, not only to generate trust between the military establishments of the two countries, but also for many other reasons, including the fact that its future naval presence in Indian Ocean could be assumed to be inevitable. The biennial series of joint exercises with PLA Navy held alternately in Chinese and Indian waters since November 2003 (with the latest having been conducted off Qingdao in April 2007)[22] has been effective as a CBM and need to be continued.

As in case of regional littorals, the engagement of extra-regional powers though maritime forces also bears attendant politico-diplomatic dividends. These may be intangible, but nonetheless important for India that seeks an increasing role in the international system. Even at this nascent stage of New Delhi's growing political ties with Washington (reinforced by an intensifying military-to-military relationship), the potential advantages for India are becoming discernable. Hence, a structured plan needs to be made for military diplomacy, prioritising the engagement of various countries. Furthermore, a plan specific to the Navy cannot be 'stand-alone' but should integrated with and form part of the overall plan for the Indian Army and Indian Air-force.

Mission-based Imperatives: Review & Recommendations

Imperative No. 1: Coastal/Port Security

After withdrawal of Indian Peace-keeping Force (IPKF) from Sri Lanka in early 1990, Indian Navy instituted Operation *Tasha* in June of that year. It involved heightened vigil along the Tamil Nadu coast and patrolling in Palk Strait to prevent cross-coast movement linked to LTTE activities. In the wake of the 1993 Mumbai bomb blasts, the Navy launched a similar operation codenamed *Swan* against seaward intrusion of anti-national elements across the Maharashtra[23] coast. Later in the mid-1990s, following the increased LTTE-linked violence in Sri Lanka, Indian Coast Guard began an operation codenamed *Nakabandi* in August 1996 in Palk Bay and Gulf of Mannar to check the influx of refugees into India. After the first-ever air-strike by LTTE (on a Sri Lankan airbase) in March 2007[24] and the increased attacks on Indian fishermen, Indian Navy (and Air Force) decided to install radars along the Tamil Nadu coast.[25] The Navy also deployed unmanned aerial vehicles (UAV) and increased the number of patrol vessels in the intervening waters. The aforesaid indicates that coastal security measures have thus far been essentially 'reactive', rather than 'anticipatory'. Such an approach may be inadequate to respond to future threats.

Some measures are being taken to adapt to the imperatives of coastal security. With Coast Guard having become the lead intelligence agency for coastal borders,[26] the responsibility for all these operations is being transferred to it from the Navy. Also, in May 2005, an Integrated Coastal Security Plan was worked out, which entails setting up of marine police stations with suitable patrol assets under jurisdiction of coastal (provincial) states.[27] Under the plan, as many as 12 police stations will be set up in Maharashtra and Tamil Nadu, with other states having a lesser number of police stations, proportionate to the length of their coastlines. The plan also envisages a greater coordination among marine police, Coast Guard and Navy. However, these measures may not suffice until coastal security remains the principal responsibility of the Coast Guard (notwithstanding that the title of the force suggests otherwise). Like in case of the Navy in the past, coastal operations will tie down the Coast Guard for tasks, which can be discharged more effectively by maritime agencies that have a better interface with law-enforcement on land. Besides, like the navy, most of the Coast Guard's policing assets have deeper drafts (depth of the underwater portion of a vessel) unsuitable for shallow-water operations close to the coast. Therefore, in a phased manner, the task of coastal security (viz. in the 12 nm territorial waters) must be devolved to the 'marine police' and law-enforcement mechanisms of the respective coastal states, with the Coast Guard (and Navy, if necessary) providing support further out at sea. (In any case, the effectiveness if coastal security will depend much on how effectively activities can be regulated in the maritime zones beyond territorial waters).

The marine police of states, in conjunction with the Coast Guard, will also be required to inspect 'suspicious' shipping on intelligence inputs before these enter Indian ports. Besides acquiring suitable and adequate patrol vessels, this will necessitate training of the marine police personnel and regular exercises in conducting VBSS (Visit Board, Search and Seizure) operations, jointly with the Coast Guard and the Navy. For such operations, the marine police will also need the expertise and equipment for detection of Nuclear, Biological and Chemical (NBC) agents.

Imperative No. 2: Regulation of Maritime Zones

As noted in Chapter 4, regulation of activities in maritime zones is crucial for India to safeguard its vital economic interests (resources, offshore assets and vessels involved in economic and scientific activities), choking nourishment to non-state actors causing internal insecurities (both within India and its maritime neighbours), and protection of marine environment. The ability to monitor and respond to disasters involving human lives and property in the area is also an important obligation, both normative and as part of international conventions that India has chosen to be part of.

The foremost imperative for this, as also noted earlier, will be achieving MDA. In context of regulating maritime zones, this will necessitate effective surveillance by airborne sensors and long-range coastal radars. These inputs could be supplemented by voluntary[28] ship-reporting (by transiting foreign vessels revealing their identity) to Indian authorities. It will also involve real-time sharing of the compiled surface picture among the command nodes of Navy, Coast Guard and concerned marine police, and down their respective command chains. In addition, it will necessitate lateral communication of actionable intelligence between the maritime forces and other government agencies like the police forces and intelligence organisations. It will also be necessary to have adequate policing assets at sea for investigation of suspicious 'contacts' and executing other tasks as required, beside maritime 'presence' and deterrence.

The primary security responsibility of India's maritime zones beyond the territorial waters will need to rest with the Coast Guard, and its Charter of duties will have to be amended accordingly. While the seaward extent of this responsibility is presently the 200 nm EEZ boundary, this will eventually be extended beyond it, depending upon the LCS allocated to India. Of course, even at present, the Coast Guard area of responsibility for Search and Rescue (SAR) extends much beyond to EEZ, since the force is the co-ordinating authority in the maritime SAR region assigned to India. As opposed to the 2.2 square kilometres of its EEZ, the Indian SAR Region encloses a sea-area of 4.6 square kilometers. However, the Coast Guard's air-surveillance and policing capacities are grossly inadequate for the envisaged tasks. While it possesses a limited number of short-range aircrafts for coastal surveillance, it has no medium-range assets. Besides, due to force level constraints, it is capable of patrolling only up to about 30 nm from the coast,[29] and even within this distance, the responsibility for the protection of offshore oil installations rests with the Navy.[30] Owing to these reasons, the Navy has been compelled to maintain a high proportion of 'brown-water' constabulary assets (about 60 per cent) in its force-mix. The Coast Guard has sought a revision of its *Perspective Plan 2002-2017*, now projecting a force-level of 268 ships (including six for "deep-sea" patrolling) and 113 aircraft (including 11 for medium-range surveillance), besides Unmanned Aerial Vehicles (UAV) and other assets.[31] Although the exact numbers necessary will need to be worked out by the government in accordance with established procedures, there is a dire need for a substantial augmentation of force-levels, which should include long-endurance ("deep-sea") patrol vessels, medium-range aircraft, aerostats and OTH (Over The Horizon) radars. As this is achieved in a phased manner, the proportion of Navy's policing assets could be reduced, but maintaining sufficient numbers to provide the optimum Navy-Coast Guard 'overlap', besides a few with adequate endurance for constabulary tasks beyond Indian maritime zones, as may be required.

The responsibility of preservation of marine environment is entrusted entirely to Coast Guard. Responding to oil-spill pollution is the most challenging of these tasks. Although *National Oil Spill Disaster Contingency Plans* have been worked out, the Coast Guard currently has capability to combat oil pollution only up to 10,000 tons (Tier-2). There is a need to upgrade this capability to more than 10,000 tons (Tier-3). Towards this, three 3,300-ton specialised pollution control vessels are being built at the Surat-based ABG Shipyard; the first one was launched in March 2007.[32] Reportedly, India has also recently developed a mathematical model for satellite-based detection and monitoring of oil-spills, which would lead to a significant spatial enhancement of its response capability.[33]

For voluntary reporting by international commercial shipping transiting Indian waters, India has had the *Indian Ship Position and Information Reporting System* (INSPIRES) for the past ten years. However, since this system is based on Very/ Ultra High Frequency (V/UHF, line-of-sight) radio link, it has a severe range limitation (about 8-10 nm from the coast). Reportedly, India plans to implement a longer-range satellite-based national *Automatic Identification System* (AIS), which would require ships to automatically transmit information periodically to receiving stations dispersed along the entire Indian coast, and thereby enable monitoring of shipping activity up to 50 nautical miles from its coast.[34] Besides assisting in vessel traffic management, SAR and pollution control, it will provide valuable inputs to enable Indian security agencies to sift suspicious maritime activity from legitimate shipping.

However, this project is still in conceptual stage and will need to be prioritised.

There are three specific areas in India's maritime zones that necessitate a greater attention. In order of the current *inter se* priority, the first comprises of the waters adjoining northern Sri Lanka. In February 2006, India formalised a 'coordinated' naval patrol arrangement with Sri Lanka, which began in 2005 to ensure safety of fishermen and to prevent criminals from crossing the maritime boundary.[35] After a series of incidents in March 2007 such as seizures of LTTE-bound material, firing on Indian fishermen (Chapter 3), and LTTE's air attacks on Sri Lanka's Katunayake Air Force Base (mentioned in the previous sub-section), these patrols were intensified.[36] However, since August 2006, the Sri Lankan government has been seeking India's assistance to enforce a sea-blockade of LTTE's military supplies.[37] This implies involving Indian maritime forces to cordon off the entire LTTE-held coastline and upgrading the existing arrangement from 'coordinated' to 'joint' patrols. Although India declined this proposal in November 2006,[38] it may be in India's long term interest to choke LTTE's lifelines, considering that the violence and instability in the island-state (and thereby in Indian waters) will grow in direct proportion to the *Tamil Tigers*' military capabilities. It is pertinent to mention that the first air attack, ever by a non-state actor in March 2007, was enabled by LTTE's access to aircraft, smuggled in a dismantled condition on LTTE-owned merchant ships.[39]

The second important area is the one adjoining Pakistan, which is essentially complicated due to the outstanding dispute over the sea boundary and New Delhi's political dissonance with Islamabad. Lately, some cooperative endeavours have succeeded, such as the October 2005 Memorandum of Understanding (MoU) between the Pakistan Maritime Security Agency (MSA) and the Indian Coast Guard. It provided for a 'hot-line' between the top commanders of the two forces (set up in November 2006) and periodic meetings between the two sides to address issues of EEZ violations, Search and Rescue (SAR) and marine pollution.[40] The latest meeting was held in August 2007.[41] While these are appropriate as initial steps towards preventing harassment of fishermen straying across the maritime boundary, it would need a further movement ahead accompanied with more CBMs.

The third area is northern Bay of Bengal/Andaman Sea. As noted in the previous chapter, regulation of activities in these waters is necessary not only for security of A&N Islands, but also to stymie choke the nourishment to insurgents operating in India's north-eastern (provincial) states. This can be done effectively using the A&N island chain. The same is examined in the following sub-section.

Imperative No. 3: Security of Island Territories

As noted in the previous chapter, while low-intensity threats to India's remote islands are more dominant, military threats to these territories in the coming decades cannot be discounted. This is particularly so in case of the A&N Islands, for which, it is essential to maintain credible deterrence. With aim of strengthening security of A&N Islands, in October 2001, India set up its first joint-service Andaman and Nicobar Command (ANC) at Port Blair. This has led to enhanced maritime security in the EEZ off the Islands since it was followed by the induction of four naval Fast Attack Craft (FAC) to supplement the existing Coast Guard patrol vessels and naval amphibious vessels. These FACs contributed substantially towards reducing unlawful acts in these waters since their high speed could enable the vessels to respond quickly to any suspicious activity that were detected in the widely scattered islands. In case of poaching by foreign fishermen for example, the detention figures of 64 boats and 646 poachers in 2000 reduced in 2002 to 38 and 271 respectively.[42] (Photograph 3)

Source: Cdr GS Khurana

Photograph 3: ***The 'Catch' off A&N Islands*****: Sharks, Sea-Cucumbers & Fishermen**

With the acquisition of the Israeli UAVs in 2002, maritime surveillance was improved further. These also proved useful to locate victims following the December 2004 *Tsunami* disaster.[43]

However, considering the extensive spread of the archipelago, the surveillance and policing assets at the disposal of ANC are presently inadequate and need to be augmented.

The few naval and coast guard *Dornier* aircraft based at Port Blair have an endurance of only about four hours. Two of the four FACs (the 'work-horses' of the ANC Flotilla) have since been gifted to Maldives and Seychelles and the other naval vessels are old and too slow. None of the patrol vessels have integral aviation (helicopters), which is needed for preliminary investigation of suspicious boats in the sea area around the vessel on patrol, before the boarding operations are launched from the vessel. Also, there are no shallow-draft vessels or hovercraft suitable for operations close to the coast. These are particularly essential since much of the coastal waters are poorly charted and the charted depths in most of the other areas have changed since 2004 when the *Tsunami* struck these islands. He planned radar network across the island chain data-linked real-time to Joint Operations Centre at Port Blair and units at sea also needs to be put on fast track.

Some cooperative arrangements with maritime neighbours have also significantly contributed towards regulating maritime activities in the area. These include coordinated naval patrolling with Indonesia along the common maritime boundary since 2002,[44] and a similar agreement with Thailand since 2006[45] (See Map 14). Such patrol arrangements could be established with Myanmar and Bangladesh too, which would be necessary to choke the flow of drugs and arms to insurgents in India's north-eastern states and the internal violence that plagues India's neighbours in the east. Backing such coordinated patrols with intelligence-sharing can prove extremely useful, as in case of *Operation Poorab* conducted by Indian armed forces, when specific information was provided by Myanmar.[46] These patrols will also serve to curb illegal migration into A&N Islands.

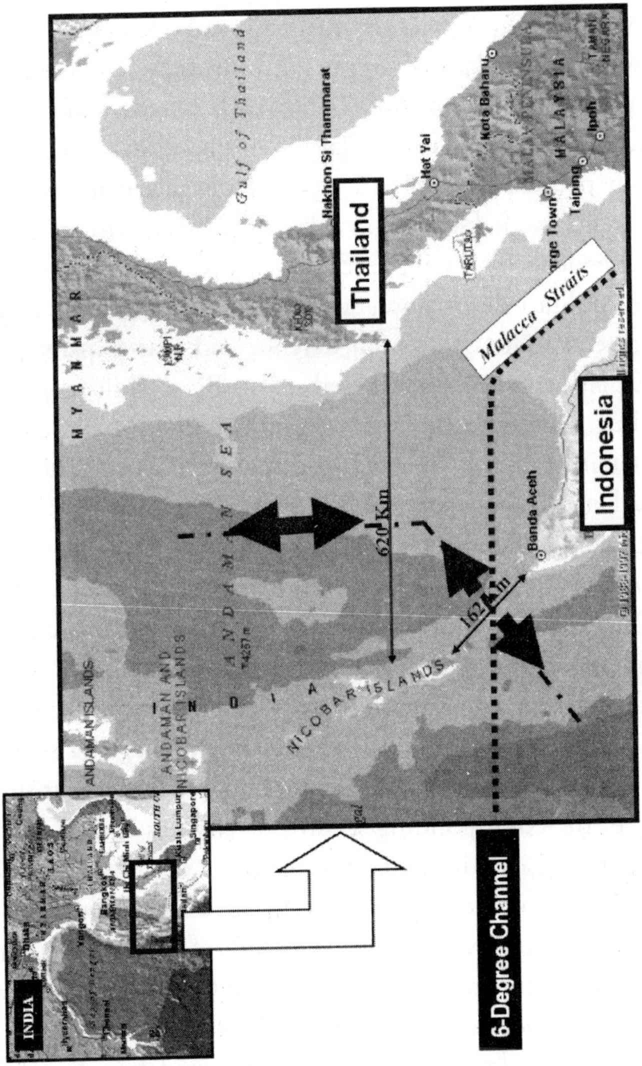

Source: Cdr GS Khurana

Map 14: Coordinated Patrols with Indonesia & Thailand

As for military preparedness of A&N Islands, the 2001 formation of ANC was not of much significance except in symbolic terms and as a successful experiment in terms of the applicability of joint-service theatre command concept in Indian conditions. Due to lack of support infrastructure, no assets for high-end naval operations are based in A&N Islands, and instead are placed under the Eastern Naval Command headquartered in Visakhapatnam 12,000 km away. Such distance will evidently lead to an unacceptable delay in deploying warships in the event of contingencies. This void needs to be corrected for the sake of adequate military defence and deterrence for these islands. Anti-submarine Warfare (ASW), air-defence and anti-ship missile-capable platforms need to be based at Port Blair, while re-basing the policing assets to the northern and southern parts of the island-chain. For this, it would be necessary to upgrade the technical and logistics support infrastructure accordingly. Ports and airfields would also need to be developed in other parts of A&N Islands to support permanent basing of the assets.

The capabilities for amphibious operations form a critical component of the overall security of island territories. Since many decades, only one amphibious brigade is stationed in these islands, which is clearly insufficient considering the spatial dispersion of islands and the security scenario in India's maritime east. Also, the corresponding sealift capacity has been static at best (i.e. on paper). In actual terms, it has declined over the years with aging of landing craft and the attendant reduction of their operational availability. It is therefore necessary to implement the planned increase of strength of landing forces from brigade-level to division-level.[47] This will, however, need to be accompanied with a proportionate upgradation of sealift/airlift capabilities (These are examined in greater detail in the following sub-section). Such capabilities will also be essential in case of other contingencies like eviction of terrorist/insurgent groups, if these manage a 'foot-hold' in an uninhabited island. These assets could also be utilized for responding to disasters, considering that these islands are prone to volcanic activity and earthquakes.

Although the aforesaid deals only with the more vulnerable A&N Islands, many of these recommendations are applicable to *Lakshadweep* as well, particularly the need for permanent basing of policing and surveillance assets in these islands. The plan to extend the only airstrip on *Agatti* Island to the nearby *Kalpati* coral islet (through land reclamation between the 400-metre gap in between) is a step in the right direction. The runway extension from the current 4,235 feet to 7,000 feet will make the airstrip long enough for operating fighters, transport aircraft and even aerial refuellers.[48] This will enhance the security of *Lakshadweep* substantially, and to some extent, it will also increase the south-west reach of the Indian maritime forces in Indian Ocean.

Imperative No. 4: Amphibious/Out of Area (OOA) Operations

As mentioned in the foregoing sub-section, amphibious sealift is essential to defend India's far-flung and scattered islands against military and non-state threats. For this mission, the Navy has since long relied upon two (now three) 3,600-ton LST (Large), five 1,100-ton LST (Medium) and six 500-ton LCUs (Landing Craft Utility), which add up to a grossly inadequate sealift capacity (photograph 4). Besides, the LST(M)s (inducted 1976-86) and LCUs (inducted 1980-87) are too old with doubtful sustained operational availability. Further, the design of these ships is based on a dated concept of amphibious operations, which necessitates their 'beaching' on the coast to disembark

Source: Indian Navy

Photograph 4: LST-Large (left), LST-Medium (top right) & LCU (bottom right)

troops/equipment through their hinged bow-doors or ramps. The non-availability of sufficient integral airlift (helicopters) is also a major constraint. While a LST(L) can operate two medium-lift *Sea King* helicopters, it can house only one. Four of the LST(M)s have flight decks to operate only light helicopters and no hangar.

In 2007, India inducted INS *Jalashva*, the first *Landing Platform Dock* (LPD) in its naval force (photograph 5). Purchased from the US under a government-to-government sale for US $ 53.5 million, the LPD is an *Austin*-class vessel earlier in commission with the US Navy as USS *Trenton.*[49] India also purchased six ex-US Navy H-3 *Seaking* transport helicopters and four Mk-8 landing craft to be carried on INS *Jalashava.* (Reports indicate that the US also offered India a second LPD of the same class, the USS *Nashville.*[50]) By opting to operate this LPD displacing more than 16,000 tons, India rightly identified the imperative to enhance Navy's sealift (and integral

Source: http://www.navybuddies.com/ships/lpd14.htm

Photograph 5: INS *Jalashva* LPD (ex-USS *Trenton*)

airlift) capacity. The vessel not only has a significantly larger carrying capacity (900 troops with equipment and 2,000 tons of stores), but more importantly, it can carry many smaller landing/air-cushion craft within its floodable 'dock' and several helicopters on its 'platform-deck'. This will not only help the Navy to learn how to operate these complex platforms, but may also be useful for Indian shipbuilders to study its design. Plans are also reported to be on the anvil to construct new vessels in Indian shipyards based on the French *Mistral*-class design. Such assets will enable India to keep abreast of present-day concepts of amphibious warfare. For example, lessons from history make it necessary to achieve the ship-to-shore movement of landing forces in a quick 'single wave', with the 'primary vectors' remaining at stand-off distance from shore to minimise losses; and using smaller but faster craft (from within the LPD) for actual landing. Besides, to achieve a tactical advantage over the adversary, sea-borne transfer must be supplemented by airlift, commonly referred to as 'vertical envelopment'.[51]

Indian Navy took the lead in responding to the *Tsunami* that lashed the shores of Indian Ocean littorals in December

2004. During disaster-relief operations, its contribution was commendable by all standards, particularly its rapid response. Within a few hours of the disaster, without even a government directive, Indian warships were ordered by higher naval authorities to embark relief material and "sail with dispatch" towards the *Tsunami*-hit areas in India and neighbouring littorals. This led to saving the valuable time, which would have gone into the necessary but lengthy decision-making procedures at the bureaucratic and political levels. As anticipated, government 'nod' to the relief effort reached the naval authorities while the warships were in transit. During the relief operations, naval survey vessels were also used innovatively as hospital ships.

However, the *Tsunami* exposed a serious void in India's naval capabilities. Considering that the disaster-relief operation involved landing enormous amounts of heavy and bulky material like portable generators, bulldozers, cranes, construction material, medical equipment and desalination plants, the Navy realized its serious handicap in terms of its capacity for integral sealift and airlift, and thereby the dire necessity of LPD-type vessels. On the other hand, an effective use of LPDs by US Navy during the same operation amply demonstrated to the global community how such platforms could be used for benign and humanitarian missions, and are thus not necessarily tied to attainment of illegitimate military ambitions overseas.

An LPD is also an ideal command-and-control platform, and due to its inherent versatility, can be used in a variety of contingencies, which may not yet be conceivable. These will be extremely useful in case India were to undertake an OOA operation to provide security assistance to littoral states of IOR. For example, in November 1988, the Indian armed forces undertook *Operation Cactus*, which involved assisting the Maldivian government to thwart a coup attempt by a rebel group. Had the militants been more meticulous in planning, Hulule airport may not have been available to India to airlift troops to Male.[52] In this case, a LPD would have been an important enabler.

However, the acquisition of such platforms must be supplemented by rapid reaction forces. India has no dedicated naval infantry or permanent forces alike the US Marines. Even the army brigade earmarked for amphibious operations are not permanent, and are on a rotational basis.

Indian Navy will also need to be involved in UN peace-support missions overseas. Although land-forces will continue to have the primary role on such occasions, the inherent attributes of naval forces make these useful for performing important support roles. The aptitude of Indian Navy for performing these roles was amply demonstrated during the UN peacekeeping mission in Somalia (1992-94). From December 1992 to October 1993, a naval Task Force comprising a corvette, an amphibious ship and a replenishment tanker were deployed with other multinational warships for providing logistics support to land forces and patrolling/surveillance off the Somali coast.[53] The 'zenith' of naval contribution came during de-induction of the Indian Army contingent in December 1994 when the security situation in Somalia was tense. While the Western countries opted to 'wait and watch', rather than putting their fleets in 'harm's way' for safety of the contingents from developing countries, an Indian Task Force comprising of two missile frigates and a replenishment tanker sailed to Somalia as a much awaited respite for Indian troops. The situation was particularly adverse for the Indian Army battalion deployed in Kismayu, a coastal town, 240 km south-west of the capital-Mogadishu. The battalion (1 Bihar) was being coerced by Somali militants to leave all its weapons and equipment behind during the de-induction. While the Indian troops were being air/sea-lifted from Kismayu (and later from Mogadishu), India's gun-mounted helicopters undertook aerial reconnaissance and provided fire cover to meet any eventuality. Indian warships were also positioned in close proximity of Somali ports to provide Naval Gunfire Support (NGS) to the Army. The electronic warfare equipment installed on these ships not only jammed militant radio frequencies but also monitored their communication channels, thereby providing valuable information to Indian forces.[54] The UN operation in Somalia has been the only occasion so far involving Indian Navy. It may be necessary for the government to involve the Navy in such operations more frequently. The imperative for the Navy to improve its mine-countermeasures (MCM) capabilities is also applicable for such operations, when India may need to clear sea-mines in maritime choke-points, either leftover from a naval conflict or those planted by terrorists.

On occasions, India may need to assist IOR littorals, specifically for its own interests. As noted in the previous chapter, most countries/regions, from where India's energy resources are sourced or where India has acquired energy stakes, are beset by various kinds of internal instabilities. In case of a serious insecurity to its assets and personnel, India may be required to assist the host country and augment the capacity of its security forces, either through the country's request or under the UN umbrella. In case the offshore assets are threatened, Indian maritime forces will be directly involved. But even if the threat manifests on the land, Indian naval forces will be essential for such an overseas deployment of the land forces.

Imperative No. 5: Sea-line Security

"To safeguard India's mercantile marine and sea-borne trade

during peace and war" is stated as a naval mission in the Maritime Doctrine.[55] Given India's expanding trade and energy interests, this mission particularly requires the Navy to have a greater geographical reach, due to which, plans are on the anvil to reverse the ratio of its 'blue water' to 'brown water' ships from 40:60 to 60:40.[56] During a war involving India, its strategic imports would invariably be carried onboard Indian-flagged carriers and provided naval escorts. Even during wars not involving India, these measures must be taken for critical cargo in key sea-line stretches affected by a conflict, particularly in Persian Gulf, Red Sea/Gulf of Aden and (South and East) China Seas; and maritime choke-points like *Strait of Hormuz* and *Malacca Straits*. As noted in the foregoing chapter, many ships carrying Indian cargo were hit during the eight-year Iran-Iraq war. It may be conceded that providing a naval escort to each vessel carrying Indian cargo was not practical, particularly when many of these ships were flying FoC. Nonetheless, Indian-flagged vessels could have been escorted. (Besides protecting cargo, it would have accrued a significant indirect dividend for India in terms of motivating Indian ship-owners to register their ships in India). It is also necessary account for the capability of a warship providing an escort, such as in terms of its air-defence and anti-submarine capabilities. This will of course be contingent upon the current and projected anti-shipping capabilities of the potential adversaries/belligerents in the region.

As examined in Chapter 4, non-state actors are now more dominant in shaping the regional security environment, and thereby the security of mercantile shipping. A greater focus of maritime forces is thus on countering piracy and mitigating the potential of maritime terrorism. The key choke-points of *Hormuz Strait, Bab-el-Mandeb* and *Malacca Straits* are most vulnerable due to the high density of traffic. Along with Coast

Guard, the Navy's surveillance and presence missions in northern Indian Ocean do provide a measure of security. This are being augmented by monitoring stations set up (or planned) by India at key locations like Maldives[57] and Madagascar[58] to monitor mercantile traffic. Beyond the choke points, too, the Navy maintains occasional presence as a spin-off of its foreign port visits and joint exercises. However, such measures evidently cannot provide a comprehensive security cover. Securing the vastly extended sea-lines would necessitate a prohibitively large number of assets. Major war vessels and frontline surveillance aircraft cannot be used since operating costs are very high and it would lead to material degradation of sophisticated assets, while also adversely affecting their operational preparedness to perform their primary functions. Besides, international law does not permit external naval forces to patrol international straits like the *Malacca Straits*.

Inter-state cooperation for sea-line security is thus indispensable. The *Alondra Rainbow* incident of 1999 amply demonstrated its dividends. In October 1999, the hijacked Japanese vessel *MV Alondra Rainbow*, re-named by pirates as *MV Mega Rama*, was interdicted by Indian Navy and Coast Guard after a dramatic chase in Indian Ocean. It was a momentous event that also underscores India's commitment towards such joint efforts. Of even greater significance was that the Indian court trying the case sentenced each of the fourteen pirates to seven years imprisonment. This was lauded by the shipping fraternity as "a rare move by a national court to assume jurisdiction over a crime committed in international waters".[59]

To further such cooperative security in the Indo-Pacific region, on June 4, 2006, India ratified the *Regional Cooperative Agreement for Anti-Piracy* (ReCAAP), which entered into force three months later.[60] Initiated by Japan, this arrangement aims

Source: Indian Coast Guard

Photograph 6: Capture of hijacked Japanese ship MV *Alondra Rainbow*

to facilitate intelligence-exchange though an Information Sharing Centre (ISC) established in November 2006 at Singapore.[61] Since 2004, the Indian Coast Guard has been participating in the *Asia Maritime Security Initiative* (AMARSECTIVE), also initiated by Japan.[62] It seeks to garner the efforts of regional coast guards to counter non-traditional maritime threats.

The three Straits-littorals (Indonesia, Malaysia and Singapore) have initiated many steps towards security in *Malacca Straits* like the trilateral coordinated naval patrols (MALSINDO) and aerial surveillance (*Eye-in-the-Sky*). However, major impediments persist for regulating the waterway, such as the inadequate capacity of littorals, their unequal stakes in the waterway and resistance of Indonesia and Malaysia to any 'operational' assistance from any external state. While India's stake in the crucial sea-passage is increasing rapidly for its trade (including energy imports), India is virtually littoral to it due to geographical contiguity, with 'good order' in the Strait inextricably linked to security in India's maritime zones. India not only has sufficient expertise and the means to contribute to security in the Straits, but also the geographical advantage, in terms of the close proximity of its *Great Nicobar* Island to the northern entrance of the waterway (only about 150 km). During the Fifth IISS-sponsored Asia Security Summit (*Shangri La Dialogue*) held in June 2006 at Singapore, India's Defence Minister conveyed India's will to assist the littorals, and also reiterated that any such assistance would be subject to their unanimous consent.[63] It is, however, important to note that 'balance of power' considerations will weigh heavily upon the littorals' decision-making. While Washington has clearly enunciated its acceptance of India's role, Beijing may also yield if India's succeeds in engaging China. While the US keenness was expressed by the US Pacific Fleet Commander during his May 2006 visit to India,[64] the Chinese Ambassador to India had stated in October 2005 that "as far as India is concerned, we don't have any problem (with its naval ships patrolling the Straits). (He however added, "but if (the) Americans come and put their battleships there, we might worry about it.").[65] There are indicators that Japan is also amenable to India's participation in Straits-security.[66] Any Indian role will, however, need to address not only 'hard' security issues and capacity-augmentation, but also capacity-building for navigational safety and disaster management. Various avenues in that direction need to be explored. For example, India could cooperate in terms of maritime domain awareness, and provide assistance in training of the littorals' maritime forces, exchange of counter-piracy and counter-terrorism doctrines, transfer of Indian-built patrol vessels, hydrography, diving operations, oil-spill pollution response, and so on. India could also coordinate its ongoing naval patrols with Indonesia with the other two littorals through real-time communication links among the headquarters of the four states (five states if Thailand is also included) and the patrol vessels and aircraft. It could even have a joint-patrol arrangement if and when sufficient political trust is generated. Although New Delhi will still have to cater for the sensitivities of the littorals, suitable arrangements could still be worked out, such as the Indian vessels patrolling the Straits with law-enforcement officials of the littoral states embarked onboard.

Considering the importance of Persian Gulf sea-lines for India's energy imports and the fact that this region is only about 600 nm from Indian shores, India has an important role to play in its maritime security. New Delhi has clearly intensified its security interactions with the sub-regional states, as is evident from the extensive port calls and naval exercises conducted with the littorals in August 2007 (mentioned earlier). I must, however, concede that so far, these exchanges have a predominantly symbolic content. Effectively, the only multilateral security construct in waters off the Arabian Peninsula at present is through the US-led multi-national naval operations, which do not include India (See Map 15 for the area of responsibility of coalition forces). Nonetheless, since end-2004, the *International Institute for Strategic Studies* (IISS) has been convening Regional Security Summits annually for informal interactions among security establishments of regional states and key stakeholders, including on maritime security issues. During the 3rd Summit held in December 2006 (*The Manama Dialogue*), India was among the 11 extra-regional states represented.[67] In the absence of an effective multilateral security arrangement in the Gulf, this forum provides a valuable forum for exchange of perspectives. India needs to be continuously involved in the sub-region through such multilateral fora and bilateral engagement with littoral states. Iran is a power of consequence in the Gulf, whose naval ties with India have traditionally been strong. Notwithstanding the growing stakes in its relations with the USA, it may be necessary for India to maintain these links with Tehran.

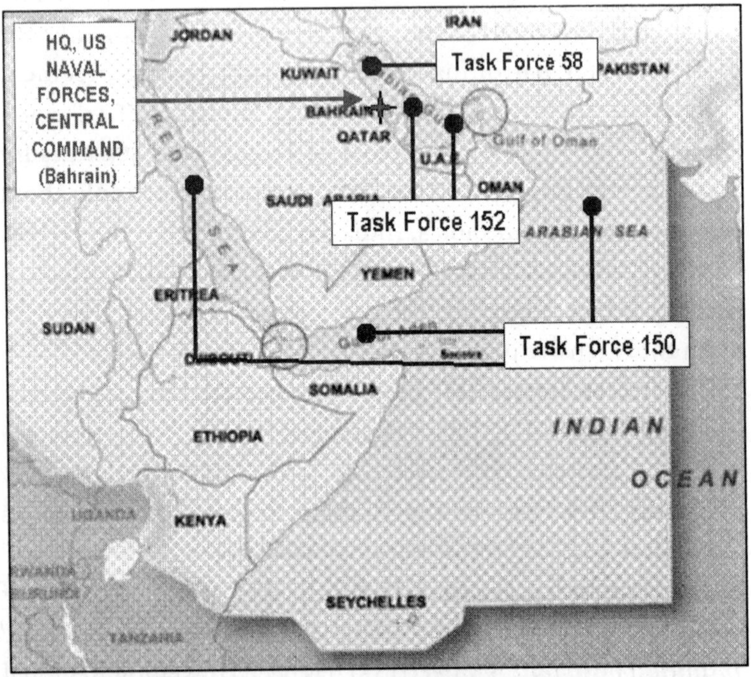

Source: http://www.cusnc.navy.mil/images/AOR.gif

Map 15: AOR of US-led Coalition Naval Forces off the Arabian Peninsula

The aforesaid indicates that security of India's sea-borne trade and commerce (including strategic imports during war) will essentially depend upon how well it can align the capabilities of its Navy for the contemporary needs and its ability to forge cooperative security bonds with the major powers and the regional states located along the sea-lines. However, another unalienable factor will be New Delhi's political will to use naval power to secure its vital interests. This leads one to a pertinent question for Indian policy-makers. In a hypothetical scenario wherein navigation across *Malacca Straits* (or *Hormuz Strait*) is impeded due to terrorist action or a military conflict, would India's maritime forces be tasked for coalition operations to keep the crucial choke-points open? It may be necessary to decide upon the responses to such questions in advance if India wishes not to be caught unawares and is thus able to take informed decisions to further its national interests.

Imperative No. 6: WMD Counter-Proliferation[68]

As noted in the previous chapter, the sea is known to be the principal medium for illegal transfers of WMDs and their means of delivery. For this purpose, the US initiated *Proliferation Security Initiative* (PSI) in May 2003 as a political commitment among "like-minded" states to counter such illegitimate transfers. Backed by intelligence sharing, it involves interdicting vessels suspected of such proliferation to terrorists and "states of concern". The PSI encountered intense opposition from many states. The majors reasons stated were that high-sea interdictions of foreign vessels are not permitted by UNCLOS. However, most states support the underlying aim of PSI since no global regime – the Nuclear Non-Proliferation Treaty (NPT) included – is tailored to prevent the terrorists' access to WMDs that has become the foremost threat to global security today. So far, probably to garner greater support of the global community, the PSI states too are not known to have carried out any "unlawful" interdictions. Instead, the US has resorted to "boarding agreements" with FoC states; thereby making efforts to maximise the portion of international shipping that Washington can 'sanitize'.

Primarily owing to India's geo-strategic location astride key sea-lines of Indian Ocean and its naval power, the US is keen for India's participation in PSI. While this is undoubtedly driven by the US' own insecurities that led to its "global war on terror", there may be a convergence – Asia is a region most beset by the insecurities of WMD proliferation, with grave ramifications for India since many of those actors (state and non-state) lie in its neighbourhood. India has had to encounter such threats in the past. In 1999, the North Korean vessel called *Kuwolsan* was seized by Indian authorities at Kandla port in Gujarat (provincial) state for a false declaration of cargo. Inspection of the ship's hold revealed Scud missiles, its components and related technical manuals, which were probably bound for Pakistan.[69] India's insecurity in this regard is also exemplified by its detention of the Iran-bound North Korean ship MV *Omrani II* in October 2006.[70]

Through PSI, India would be part of an intelligence grid, which will contribute to its maritime domain awareness. It would also help Indian Navy to foster operational-compatibility with major navies to address other security issues of common interest in the Indian Ocean. More importantly, PSI would provide a political backing, if India were to take a 'legitimate', but not a *strictly* 'legal' action in case of an impending threat to its security. To understand this, consider a hypothetical scenario – a foreign-flagged vessel is carrying WMDs to terrorists in a neighbouring state, from where these could reach India by land. The vessel's Flag-state declines to cooperate. (If bound for India, the vessel could have been legally interdicted in territorial waters). The vessel is nonetheless interdicted by India (in international waters). How does India face the global community since its action is *not legal*? The action is nevertheless *legitimate*, but this would have to be asserted. Here, PSI's political backing would be necessary when India's insists that its own security is linked to that of its neighbourhood. Through this, one may derive other dividends too. If India is a PSI-state, other participants are more likely to act on a proliferation case that affects India even if it does not imperil them. A significant advantage of PSI is that it is not a treaty. It would generate only a broad political obligation, not legal commitments, thus providing India the flexibility to act on a case-to-case basis as dictated by national interests.

Participation in the initiative is unlikely to entail a financial burden for the state, apart from the sunk costs of maintaining intelligence infrastructure, law-enforcement mechanism and military assets, which may be tasked as decided by the government. On the other hand, joint interdiction exercises/ operations would improve India's naval capabilities through interaction with other navies rather than degrade them, as is often feared. Participation in PSI would also enable the navy to realise its politico-diplomatic role, which is discussed later.

Given that PSI 'Statement of Interdiction' principles clearly rule out interdiction of foreign-flagged vessels on high seas (in conformity with UNCLOS), the primal reason for India's non-participation in PSI has been that the initiative is not *explicitly* backed by the UN. However, in the coming years, New Delhi may need to involve itself in coalition operations outside the ambit of UN mandate, which are not in contradiction with the purposes and principles of the UN Charter. In this direction, the statement of Indian Defence Minister AK Antony regarding India's policy on military deployment overseas is notable. During his address to the army commanders in April 2007, he acknowledged the need for "involvement of Armed Forces – not necessarily under the aegis of the UN – in resolving ongoing conflicts and defusing international tensions."[71] Besides, the UN Secretary General's high-level panel report of 2004 has recommended PSI rather clearly, saying that "We believe that all States should be encouraged to join this voluntary initiative."[72]

India's wariness may also be based on the view that PSI contravenes the UN Charter in terms of its laws regarding the use of force in international relations. Article 51 of the Charter bestows states only with "the right of individual or collective self-defence… if an armed attack occurs". At best, this can be extended to the right of *Anticipatory Self-defence* if the materialization of threat is imminent, provided the use of force is limited by two important principles, 'necessity' and 'proportionality'.[73] On the other hand, PSI's thrust is on *Preventive Self-defence* (ie. when there is no evidence that actualization of the threat is imminent), thereby contradicting the prevailing international law. However, it is important to note that legal regimes are 'dynamic' and not 'engraved in stone'. For example, in 2004, the UN Security Council Resolution 1540 created a precedent of the UN's role in preventing WMD proliferation. The resolution requires all states to reinforce domestic laws and tighten export and border controls to prevent such proliferation to non-state actors. While it does not explicitly authorize use of force, very significantly, for the first time, Chapter 7 of the UN Charter has been evoked *without any evidence that the manifestation of a threat is imminent.*[74]

The *Container Security Initiative* (CSI) is another global security arrangement against WMD terrorism. Launched by the US in January 2002, it involves a bilateral understanding of the

US with other countries to station customs officials in each other's ports and use of advanced technology for "non-intrusive" detection of illegal cargo that may be concealed in shipping containers. 59 ports (in 27 countries) worldwide have joined the initiative. These include Dubai, Colombo, Port Klang, Tanjung Pelepas and Singapore in Indian Ocean (and its contiguous straits). Two Chinese ports, Shanghai and Shenzen, are also CSI-compliant. India is also in an advanced stage of discussions with the US to join the Initiative, which may make Nhava Sheva of Mumbai the 60th CSI-compliant port. Although CSI primarily involves port authorities, customs and intelligence agencies, the marine police responsible for port security would also have an important role.

Initially, CSI was a conundrum for many countries that had the USA as a major export destination. India was one of these. On the one hand, there were security and sovereignty concerns attendant to stationing of US officials in their ports (notwithstanding that CSI is a reciprocal arrangement). Besides, compliance with CSI-standards would have entailed enormous financial investment for advanced technology and port-operations, besides time delays due to container checks. On the other hand, if their ports were not CSI-compliant, their exports would have to be re-routed through trans-shipment ports that were CSI-compliant, which would have led to delays and possibly even disruptions due to congestion in these few ports. This would have resulted in increase of costs and ensuing losses, including in terms of competitiveness.

It was however realised eventually that CSI-participation would be advantageous in commercial terms due to increased 'attractiveness' of their ports owing to reduced risk and greater insurance value, particularly in the possible event of heightened tension due to a terrorist attack on maritime trade. Furthermore,

CSI was unlikely to adversely affect efficiency of cargo movement as believed hitherto, since containers usually await loading at the port of origin and this period could be utilized for inspecting them, rather than on arrival at US ports.

In terms of CSI, India must look 'beyond the horizon'. New Delhi's motivation to join the initiative has largely been economic, which is understandable considering that the USA is India's largest trading partner. However, there are security dividends for India as well. This will improve India's container security apparatus, thereby enabling Indian ports to sanitize imports. Furthermore, CSI is currently a bilateral 'hub-and-spokes' mechanism envisaged to cater for security of the "US homeland". In future however, it may become necessary for countries like India plagued by terrorism to have similar arrangements with key countries from where their imports are sourced. CSI thus bears a potential to be expanded beyond from its present US orientation to a global 'web', when it could even serve as another tool for WMD counter-proliferation.

Imperative No. 7: Warfighting/Conventional Deterrence

Sea-control capability is necessary for India to achieve its operational objectives during a military conflict in a regional context. Aircraft Carrier operations would be integral to such a doctrine. With INS *Viraat* (the only carrier presently in commission) due to be de-commissioned soon, it has become rather exigent for INS *Vikramaditya* (the refurbished Russian carrier *Admiral Gorshkov*) to be inducted (photograph 7), supplemented by the indigenous carrier called Air Defence Ship (ADS) being constructed at Cochin Shipyard Ltd. (CSL), Kochi. The day the first ADS is successfully operationalized will truly be a watershed in Indian warship building capability. India's naval forces will need to be structured on, at least, two *operational* carriers. In case of a military conflict, one can be dedicated for missions in direct support of the war, and the other further out at sea to provide air-defence to strategic commercial shipping.

Source: Wikipedia

Photograph 7: Russian Aircraft Carrier *Admiral Gorshkov* (to be INS *Vikramaditya*)

In present times, *battle-space dominance* is indispensable for achieving sea-control, which will be further contingent upon MDA through C[4]ISR (examined in beginning of this chapter). For ISR, real-time satellite imagery will be a crucial force-multiplier in future wars, towards which, Indian technology has covered substantial ground. However, this cannot supplant the imperative to fill India's gaping void in terms of air-borne surveillance. As also mentioned earlier, communication networking of information (C[4]) among dispersed units is being addressed through projects like NEWN. Net-work Centric Warfare (NCW) will not only hasten decision-making at various levels in chain of command, but also reduce risk of errors by eliminating imponderables. Achieving contemporary standards of C[4] indigenously may not be too difficult considering that its core, i.e. Information Technology (IT) is the strength of Indian industry. Hence, a partnership between *Defence Research and Development Organisation* (DRDO) and private industries has immense potential in this direction.

High-end ASW capabilities are expected to be critical to cater for underwater threats in the short-to-medium timeframe. As noted in beginning of the chapter, MDA is commonly understood to address the surface and air dimensions of maritime operations. In Indian context however, there is a dire necessity to include the underwater dimension as well. The capabilities of ASW aircraft (which can also be used long-range surface surveillance) urgently need to be bolstered. While some platforms have been upgraded qualitatively, all are aging and grossly inadequate in numbers. Besides, conventional means of subsurface surveillance need to be supplemented by sea-bed sensors (deployable in choke-points/ critical areas) and non-acoustic means of submarine detection. Besides ISR, it will also be required to disseminate the compiled underwater picture and threat assessment across all units and command nodes by the fastest available means (C^4).

The Navy will also have to adapt to contemporary concepts of mine counter measures (MCM). Neutralization of the enemy's 'intelligent' mines will need to be through 'mine-hunting' sonars and remotely-operated-vehicles (ROV), rather than 'mine-sweeping'. The latter concept employing wire-cutters, magnetic sweeps and noise-makers is only suitable against older mines, most of which are obsolete today. The Navy has placed orders on Goa Shipyard (India) for eight MCM vessels (with mine-hunting gear being acquired from foreign sources).[75] The type of gear to be installed is not yet known, but even if it meets the criteria to hunt modern mines, these vessels may be numerically inadequate to defend India's many vital ports and harbours that dot its extensive coastline, let alone being made available for OOA operations.

Naval forces have always been employed in support of land wars such as to effect a blockade or during amphibious assaults. However, technological advances have made the naval contribution more significant and almost decisive in the outcome of war, as was demonstrated by the standoff precision strikes by the US forces during Gulf Wars. During the 2002 *Operation Enduring Freedom*, its sea-based *Tomahawk* land-attack cruise missiles (LACM) struck Taliban assets more than a thousand miles inland, virtually turning Afghanistan into a littoral. The Indian Maritime Doctrine also aptly factors it, but the technological void is serious, though not conspicuous. For example, *BrahMos* is an excellent cruise missile for anti-ship strikes, but it is vastly inferior to the *Tomahawk* as a LACM, particularly due to its maximum range and terminal homing facilities.

The aforesaid example of extended range LACM is equally relevant in the context of India's conventional deterrence. In order to deter coercion/compellence or intervention by a major naval power, India's minimal sea-control capabilities would have sufficed two decades back. However, the inclusion of technological 'force-multipliers' in inventory of major powers today places new demands on Navy to achieve a credible conventional deterrence. In other words, in this hi-tech era of extended-range littoral warfare, India's security perimeter would need to be expanded accordingly.

Imperative No. 8: Strategic Deterrence

Strategic deterrence is among the foremost of India's security imperatives, since it continues to be a guarantor of an independent foreign policy. India needs a nuclear triad with a sea-based element, which would significantly reduce the probability of an adversary destroying its nuclear weapons in a first strike. In other words, India needs a second-strike capability, which can best be provided by a submarine. Although its relevance is greater for India considering its 'no-first-use' policy, India is the only one among major world powers without a sea-based deterrent.

Reports indicate that India is acquiring two *Akula II*-class nuclear submarines (SSN) from Russia on lease for five years. Armed with *Klub-S* cruise missiles capable of carrying nuclear warheads, these will be an interim arrangement in that direction.[76] However, with the 300 km maximum range of the *Klub-S*, this SSN will hardly be an effective deterrent against China, even if it is positioned in western Pacific with high attendant risks. The same is the case with submarine-launched version of the 250-350 km range ballistic missile Project K-15 (variant of *Prithvi*/ *Dhanush*), which is being developed by India's DRDO.[77] An appropriate deterrent therefore necessitates an early fructification of indigenous Advanced Technology Vessel (ATV), currently projected to be ready for induction by 2011,[78] and its *Sagarika* long-range nuclear missile project.

Imperative No. 9: Politico-Diplomatic Functions

An important role of naval forces is to serve as diplomatic instruments to further the state's political objectives and foreign policy, as part what is referred to as military diplomacy. A warship at sea is particularly suitable for this task, broadly due to its three attributes. Firstly, it is capable of operating in international waters on a sustained basis, both in peace and in war. Secondly, its operational flexibility enables it to alter its military posture in a graduated manner to convey the political message appropriate to the need. Thirdly, under a stringent command chain, its actions are highly 'controllable' by political leadership.

Naval diplomacy offers a wide range of options to support national objectives. On the most benign end of the spectrum is use of naval sea-going units to radiate the state's soft power, such as through a 'goodwill' visit by a warship to a foreign port. While it also showcases the country's military power, more importantly, it represents the nation in its entirety and renews the relationship of its people with those in the foreign land. For people of Indian nationality or descent living in the port being visited, it is a prized occasion that rekindles emotional bonds. Many a time, foreign ship visits lead to (or are indicators of) strengthening political ties. A pertinent example is Myanmar. The port calls of Indian naval ships to Myanmar have increased since the first visit of one submarine and two destroyers at Yangon port in December 2002. In September 2003, and again in December 2005, warships of the two states even carried out basic joint exercises at the culmination of such port calls. These visits have contributed substantially to a closer relationship between the two states, as is evident by the vigour of high-level visits, and very significantly, the participation of a Burmese corvette at *Milan-2006* in Port Blair (discussed later), which is the first time in four decades that a Burmese warship visited any foreign port.[79]

Naval assets could also be tasked to assist the foreign country, which will lead to building political trust. The occasions when Indian Navy has been involved in such diplomacy has been steadily rising – it includes sea-front security for Mozambique during the African Union Summit in at Maputo in 2003 and assistance to Mauritius and Maldives in training EEZ surveillance and hydrographic survey on various occasions.[80] Assistance could also be in the form of hardware supplies, as a gift or at 'friendship' price. In June 2005, India provided 150 tonnes of critical spare-parts to Vietnam for its Russian-origin naval ships.[81] The Indian-built Fast Attack Crafts, (*Tarmugli* and *Tillanchang*) were gifted to the maritime forces of Seychelles and Maldives, respectively.[82]

As discussed in preceding part of this chapter, navies have a major role during natural disasters to provide humanitarian assistance. During the December 2004 *Tsunami*, the relief operations undertaken by Indian Navy not only earned India the gratitude of Indonesia, Sri Lanka and Maldives, but made global community take notice of it. More recently in May 2006, Indian Navy (and Air Force) responded again to the earthquake in Indonesia, again making a major contribution to the relief effort. However, the Indian response could have been more prompt in such a contingency, where time lost is directly proportional to lives lost. It was unfortunate that the date of occurrence of disaster (26 May 2006) coincided with the Indian Defence Minister's visit to Japan and China, which led to a delay of nearly two days before his directions translated into launch of Operation *Marham*.[83] There may, therefore, be a need to incorporate redundancies in the command chain and institute arrangements and standard operating procedures (SOP) to enable appropriate and quick action in the event of such disasters.

To assuage to apprehensions of regional states following India's acquisition of major naval power-projection assets in late-1980s, India began conducting a congregation of regional navies at Port Blair called "*Milan*" (Meeting). Since the first one held in 1995, this biennial event has succeeded in building trust through increased transparency. Furthermore, the seminars and joint-exercises connected with the week-long event not only bear a professional value, but are accompanied by greater interactions and sharing of perceptions among participants. The success of *Milan* motivated the conduct of a similar congregation at Mumbai in 2001, but on a much larger scale called the International Fleet Review (IFR-2001). The scope of *Milan* could be further increased by organising the event biennially (or even annually) on the west coast, wherein West Asian and African navies could be invited.

The increasing number of naval exercises being conducted by India jointly with other countries, either as part of naval congregations and port-calls, or the structured ones with friendly states and major powers is also aimed to further its foreign policy, besides the operational objectives. Another significant trend has been conduct of such exercises away from Indian waters. For example, what began in 2000 as basic naval manoeuvres with Vietnam in the South China Sea, had graduated in 2007 to 'promiscuous' naval interactions with Japan, US, China, Vietnam, the Philippines, Singapore, New Zealand in the western Pacific. The joint exercises with France (in Red Sea)[84] and Russia (off Vladivostok)[85] in 2007 are other examples. While such exercises were essential for India for providing familiarity and experience to its Navy to operate in the seas that were hitherto 'alien', this will enable joint operations in these waters and thereby further the process of strengthening political ties with these states. Also notable is the symbolic message to global community that the geographical reach of India's naval forces is increasing, which has its own accompanying politico-diplomatic dividends.

Joint peace-support operations under UN mandate, though a normative contribution of a major power towards global peace and security, also forms an important element of military diplomacy. Indian Navy's role as part of the UN operation in Somalia (1992-94) mentioned earlier (*Imperative 4*) was a significant contribution in this direction. Considering that it was the first time in history of UN peacekeeping that a naval task force from any developing country had been deployed for such a major task, its symbolic import is undeniable. In his narrative of the de-induction phase, an army officer of the Indian contingent in Somalia recalls, "At the crack of dawn on December 6 (1994), hundreds of local residents…women and children thronged the silvery shores of Kismayu (Somalia's coastal town), many waving out to the ships shouting '*Hindiya, Hindiyan sheeps*!' ('India, Indian ships'). As for the officers and men of the Indian Brigade…it was a moment of pride, (and) elation…" He adds, "local residents were quite used to seeing the US and massive European naval ships plying off the shores of Somalia. This was the first time that they had seen such large battleships from a Third World [sic] country. They were further surprised to learn that the Indian battleships were made in India. The Indian naval ships in Somalia boosted India's image overseas considerably".[86]

On the other end of a navy's diplomatic-role-spectrum is gunboat diplomacy. The concept may be despised within the comity of nations, but it still remains one of the options to preserve supreme national interests. This has often been used by major powers, with the most recent example being the deployment of second carrier battle group by the US in February 2007 to compel Iran to abandon its nuclear 'ambitions'.[87] India, too, has engaged in gunboat diplomacy against Pakistan during the 1999 Kargil conflict (Operation *Vijay*), wherein the Western Fleet, supplemented by five warships from Eastern Fleet, were mobilised (in complete readiness) and deployed in northern Arabian Sea. During signing of the Indo-Sri Lankan accord on 29 July 1987, two Indian frigates were sent to Colombo on personal request of President Jayawardene. It was meant to be a symbolic expression of India's solidarity with him to dissuade a coup attempt. Two years later, the Indian aircraft carrier INS *Viraat* (with one infantry battalion and Marine Commandoes embarked) was deployed off Sri Lankan coast under an operation codenamed *Jupiter*. Following President Premadasa's truce with the LTTE and his abrupt order for IPKF withdrawal, this was necessary to deter any action by Sri Lankan Armed Forces against IPKF and as an indicator of India's resolve to continue the IPKF deployment.[88] For India to continue maximising its foreign policy options, it must be capable of practising gunboat diplomacy. The requirement to build naval capabilities for this would evidently be concurrent with that to prevent such compellence by an extra-regional power. Filling critical voids in India's blue water capabilities would close the gap with major powers and widen it relative to regional states.

Imperative No. 10: Security of Indians Abroad

Protection of interests of Indians abroad is another essential element of India's foreign policy, first articulated by Pandit Jawaharlal Nehru; as early as in December 1947 during his address to the Constituent Assembly. He said, "we cannot protect any vested interests (of Indians abroad), which injure the cause of the country they are in...Nevertheless undoubtedly we shall try to do our best to protect all (their) *legitimate* (emphasis added) interests." The protection of the lives and property of its citizens overseas therefore evidently falls within the ambit of this guiding foreign policy articulation, and could be another mission, for which the Navy may be tasked. This can also be seen as an extension of its politico-diplomatic role mentioned in the previous sub-section.

For many years since independence, however, Indian policy

did not lay stress on this imperative, and it only the events of 1990s that indicate India's realisation of the 'worth' of its nationals abroad. During the 1991 Gulf War, more than one hundred thousand Indians were flown back to India from Kuwait. The involvement of Navy began more recently. In April 2006, it was directed to bring home ten Indian sailors stranded in Seychelles for over six months. After their Iraqi-flagged vessel was ransacked by pirates, the ship-owner had disowned the vessel along with its crew.[89] In July 2006, following the Israeli military offensive against Palestinian guerrillas in Lebanon, the Navy launched Operation *Sukoon*, evacuating more than 2,000 people (mostly Indians, but significantly, also nationals of Sri Lanka, Nepal and Lebanon) from Lebanon to Cyprus, from where, they were flown to India.[90] However, there have also been cases wherein India has vacillated. For example, following the February 2006 hijacking of the Indian dhow *Bhaktisagar* off Somalia for ransom, the Navy had worked out plans for the rescue of its crew.[91] Mobilising the permission of the Somali authorities for the operation could not have been difficult. However, the Navy was never involved and the ransom was paid. There may have been overwhelming compulsions on the Indian government, but the inference drawn from press-reports indicated an hesitancy on part of India to act, which also indicates the importance of shaping perceptions of the media.

In addition to the will of the political leadership to employ naval power at its disposal, it is also necessary for Navy to possess sufficient capabilities to discharge the task. While all warships with sufficient endurance can cater for most scenarios, the versatility of long-range sealift and integral airlift platforms like the LPDs make them highly suited to respond to most contingencies involving the security of Indians overseas, and particularly when the people have to be evacuated in large numbers due to extreme violence or lawlessness in host country (As mentioned in Chapter 3, a large number of Indians work in the IOR countries that are plagued by internal instabilities).

In this regard, the Lebanon Sealift of July 2006 (Operation *Sukoon* mentioned above) is instructive on two counts. *First,* although three Indian warships were involved in the operation (the fourth – a tanker, was not used for the sealift), these did not have sufficient capacity to accommodate all evacuees, and only a total of 2,280 people were transported. Even after the operation was terminated, about 10,000 Indians were still in Lebanon, and many of them had approached Indian embassy in Beirut for their return to India. Even for those evacuated, the ships were unable to transfer the people to India directly and instead, had to undertake shuttle trips back and forth between Beirut (Lebanon) and Larnaca (Cyprus). This entailed an avoidable delay in a situation wherein time was of critical importance. This is also accompanied with other risks, for example; what if a suitable staging point (like Larnaca) was not available? *Secondly*, due to limited space for berthing ships in Beirut port and the security risks involved, the Indian ships were permitted to dock one at a time, thus also contributing to the delay. In case a LPD was available, it would not have to dock at all. Its integral airlift capacity (the several helicopters onboard) would have enabled a quick embarkation of evacuees onto the LPD at anchorage, or cruising at safe distance from the ongoing violence. (Of course, helicopter operations would have necessitated the concurrence of Lebanese and Israeli authorities).

The Lebanon Sealift case also provides two other lessons in terms of the reaction time for such missions. *Firstly*, it was fortunate for India that the five Indian warships were on a 'goodwill' port calls in Greece at that time. If not, these would have to be dispatched from India (after stocking them up with necessary ration stores). This indicates the need for further streamlining Navy's rapid-response capabilities and organisation. Secondly, it was also fortuitous that the warships' visit to Greece ended on 13 July, 2006 i.e. only a day later after the Israeli offensive commenced. However, this chance was not capitalised on to reduce the reaction time. The government directive for the operation came four days later (17 July, 2006) when the ships had already left Mediterranean Sea (Beirut is located in eastern Mediterranean) and were transiting through Suez Canal. The ships could thus reach Beirut only on 20 July.[92] As in case of Operation *Marham* (mentioned in preceding subsection), this reiterates the necessity of a quicker decision-making at the top echelons of the government.

REFERENCES

1. Indian Maritime Doctrine, Integrated Headquarters, Ministry of Defence (Navy), April 25, 2004, p. 73.
2. NEWN is a state-of-the-art secure high-speed data network linking all units at sea with the command nodes ashore. This will enable exchange of surface and air operational picture in real-time, ie. almost instantaneously.
3. Rajat Pandit, 'Shedding the step-child tag', *Times of India*, New Delhi, March 7, 2006, p.15.
4. Christopher Cavas, 'The Thousand-Ship Navy', *Armed Forces Journal*, 2007, at http://www.armedforcesjournal.com/2006/12/2336959 (Accessed 04 Apr 07).
5. Robert Karniol, 'India woos ASEAN with exercise', *Jane's Defence Weekly*, Vol.18 (18), October 31, 1992, p. 6.
6. 'Vietnam and India establish New Strategic Partnership', *Aviation & Aerospace*, July 7, 2007, at http://www.domain-b.com/aero/july/2007/20070707_vietnam.htm (Accessed 13 Aug 07).
7. 'Vietnam and India establish New Strategic Partnership', Aviation

& Aerospace, July 7, 2007, at http://www.domain-b.com/aero/july/2007/20070707_vietnam.htm
Abdul Khalik, 'Indonesia-India security pact comes into effect', *The Jakarta Post*, April 3, 2007 at http://www.thejakartapost.com/detailworld.asp?fileid=20070403.K01 (Accessed 04 Apr 07).

8. 'PCG and Indian Coast Guard hold joint exercises', *Balita News* (Philippines news agency), June 12, 2007, at http://news.balita.ph/html/article.php/20070612145425951 (Accessed 13 Aug 07).
9. PS Suryanarayana, 'Plan to enhance maritime security – Australia backs India's policing of Indian Ocean', *The Hindu*, June 7, 2006 at http://www.hindu.com/2006/06/07/stories/2006060718251500.htm (Accessed 05 Apr 07).
10. 'Indian Navy warships off to Persian Gulf', *NDTV news*, August 9, 2007, at http://www.ndtv.com/convergence/ndtv/story.aspx?id=NEWEN20070022107&ch=8/9/2007%2010:25:00%20PM.
11. Hamid Ansari, 'Imperatives of Indian Policy in West Asia'. In NS Sisodia and C Uday Bhaskar (ed.). *Emerging India: Security and Foreign Policy Perspectives*, 2005, IDSA and Promilla & Co., New Delhi, p. 251.
12. After the Indian OPV INS *Saryu* (SLNS *Sayura*) sold in 2000, India is likely to provide Sri Lanka the Coast Guard OPV CGS *Varaha*. 'Sri Lanka: India donates second warship to Sri Lanka', *SiberNews*, February 26, 2007 at http://www.sibernews.com/news/sri-lanka/-200702267549/ (Accessed 05 Apr 07).
13. Indian warships provided escort to more than 20 American and other coalition ships carrying high value cargo through the Straits between April and September 2002 in an operation code-named "Sagittarius". See, 'Escort Operations by the Indian Navy In the Straits of Malacca, Indian Navy press release, July 16, 2002 at http://armedforces.nic.in/navy/press.htm
14. Embassy of India, Washington DC report, May 25, 2006 at http://www.indianembassy.org/newsite/induspolApr06.asp (Accessed 05 Jun 06).
15. United States Seeks Access, Berthing Rights for USN Ships at Indian Ports', *India Defence*, April 18, 2007, at http://www.india-defence.com/reports-3054 (Accessed 25 Apr 07).

16. 'Indo-US defence support agreement in final stage', *Indian Express*, July 15, 2007, p. 2.
17. John Cherian, 'A Strategic Stopover', *Frontline*, 22(10), 2005, at http://www.hinduonnet.com/fline/fl2210/stories/20050520005412300.htm (Accessed 30 Mar 07).
18. *Ministry of Defence, Government of India*, Press Release, December 15, 2006, at http://pib.nic.in/release/release.asp?relid=23377&kwd= (Accessed March 30, 2007).
19. Vivek Raghuvanshi, 'Indian Navy Exercises Strategic Capabilities', *Defence News*, April 9, 2007, at http://defensenews.com/story.php?F=2670170&C=asiapac (Accessed 13 Aug 07).
20. Gurpreet S Khurana, 'Security of Sea Lines: Prospects for India–Japan Cooperation', *Strategic Analysis* (*Routledge*), Vol. 31, No. 1, Jan–Feb 2007, p. 139.
21. 'Japanese Defence Agency upgraded to Ministry', *The Hindu*, December 15, 2006 at http://www.hindu.com/2006/12/15/stories/2006121502341800.htm (Accessed 05 Jan 07).
22. 'Navies of India, China conduct exercises off Chinese Coast', *The Hindu*, April 16, 2007, at http://www.hindu.com/thehindu/holnus/001200704161757.htm (Accessed 21 Apr 07).
23. India's (provincial) state on the west coast with its capital at Mumbai.
24. 'Tigers show they can fly as they bomb Lankan airbase', *Indian Express*, March 27, 2007, p. 1 and 2.
25. 'After LTTE air attack, IAF sets up radar near Rameshwaram', *Indian Express*, March 29, 2007, p.3 and 'Navy to install radars at seven places', *Sahara Samay*, April 4, 2007, at http://www.saharasamay.com/samayhtml/articles.aspx?newsid=72877 (Both accessed 05 Apr 07).
26. Ministry of Defence (Govt. of India) Annual report (2005-06), p. 55.
27. Upali Rupasinghe, 'India puts in place integrated coastal security plan', *Daily News*, May 30, 2005 at http://www.dailynews.lk/2005/05/30/sec02.htm (Accessed 5 Apr 07).
28. It cannot be made mandatory as per international law since it would then violate the spirit of UNCLOS-3, which is based on the principal of freedom of the seas.

29. Sudha Ramachandran, 'India moves to secure its shores', *Asia Times* online, December 22, 2006, at http://www.atimes.com/atimes/South_Asia/HL22Df01.html (Accessed 4 Apr 07).
30. Within the Navy, the task is entrusted with a 2-star Admiral appointed as the FODAG (Flag Officer, Offshore Defence Advisory Group).
31. Rajat Pandit, 'Shedding the step-child tag', *Times of India*, New Delhi, March 7, 2006, p.15.
32. 'Coast Guard launches its first pollution control vessel', Ministry of Defence (Government of India) press release, March 20, 2007 at http://pib.nic.in/release/release.asp?relid=26235 (Accessed 04 Apr 07).
33. Kounteya Sinha, 'Eyes in the sky to help detect oil spills', *Times of India*, November 17, 2006, at http://timesofindia.indiatimes.com/articleshow/461225.cms (Accessed 01 Feb 07).
34. Sandeep Dikshit, 'New system planned to monitor ships', *The Hindu*, December 1, 2006, at http://www.hinduonnet.com/2006/12/01/stories/2006120103131500.htm (Accessed 01 Feb 07).
35. RK Radhakrishnan, 'Coordinated naval patrolling formalised', *The Hindu*, February 25, 2006, at http://www.hindu.com/2006/02/25/stories/2006022509630100.htm (Accessed 05 Apr 06).
36. 'India, Sri Lanka conduct joint sea patrol to tackle threats', *The Financial Express*, March 30, 2007 at http://www.financialexpress.com/fe_full_story.php?content_id=159444 (Accessed 05 Apr 07).
37. Rajat Pandit, 'Lanka seeks India's help', *Times of India*, May 30, 2007, p.11. and 'Sri Lanka seeks military support from India', *The Times of India*, August 10, 2006, at http://timesofindia.indiatimes.com/articleshow/1879540.cms (Accessed 9 Dec 06).
38. 'India rejects Rajapakse's call for joint naval patrols – Hindu', *Tamil Net*, November 29, 2006, at http://www.tamilnet.com/art.html?catid=13&artid=20438 (Accessed 09 Dec 06).
39. Simon Gardner, 'LTTE 'air force' small, but a significant threat', *Indian Express*, March 27, 2007, p. 10.
40. MoD Annual report (2005-06), pp. 55-56 at http://mod.nic.in/reports/ (Accessed 4 Apr 07).

41. 'India, Pak to hold talks on maritime cooperation', *Times of India*, August 8, 2007, p. 11.
42. Prakash Nanda, "Strategic Significance of the Andamans", *Bharat Rakshak Monitor* – Volume 5(3) Nov-Dec 2002 at http://www.bharat-rakshak.com/MONITOR/ISSUE5-3/nanda.html (Accessed 06 Dec 03).
43. Barbara Opall-Rome, 'India Uses Israeli UAVs To Locate Tsunami Victims', *C4SIR Journal*, January 03, 2005 at http://www.c4sirjournal.com/story.php?F=580988 (Accessed 08 Mar 05).
44. Govt. of India (PIB) Press Release, December 04, 2002 at http://pib.nic.in/archieve/lreleng/lyr2002/rdec2002/04122002/r041220027.html (Accessed 07 Aug 05).
45. PS Suryanarayana, "India signs maritime accord with Thailand", *The Hindu*, May 21, 2005 at http://www.hindu.com/2005/05/21/stories/2005052104421200.htm (Accessed 05 Apr 06).
46. "Myanmar offered arms for lending a helping hand" *Hindustan Times*, September 12, 1998 at http://www.ibiblio.org/obl/reg.burma/archives/199809/msg00419.html (Accessed 05 Dec 06).
47. Rajat Pandit, 'Need to Bolster A&N Security', *Times of India*, March 25, 2007, p. 13.
48. Shiv Aroor, 'IAF game for extending Agatti airstrip', *Indian Express*, March 10, 2007, p. 12.
49. Chidanand Rajghatta, 'USS Trenton is now INS Jalashva', *Times of India*, January 19, 2007, at http://timesofindia.indiatimes.com/articleshow/1287538.cms (Accessed 05 Feb 07).
50. 'Indian Navy seeks second troop carrier from US', *India News online*, July 23, 2007, at http://news.indiamart.com/news-analysis/indian-navy-seeks-se-16244.html
51. For details of the *Trenton*-deal and India's need, see Gurpreet S Khurana, 'USS Trenton Sets Course for India: Imperatives for Navy's LPD Buy', *Defence Digest*, January-February 2006, p. 2.
52. Rahul Roy-Chaudhury. *Sea power and Indian Security*. Bressey's, London & Washington, 1995, pp. 141-143.
53. 'UN Peacekeeping', Indian Navy website, at http://indiannavy.nic.in/somalia.htm (Accessed 16 Aug 07).
54. Colonel Anil Shorey, 'The Naval Saga in Somalia', *Ministry of*

Defence (*Government of India*) website, March 1, 2006, at http://www.mod.nic.in/samachar/march1-06/h2.htm (Accessed 05 Apr 07).

55. Indian Maritime Doctrine, Integrated Headquarters, Ministry of Defence (Navy), April 25, 2004, p. 101.
56. "Indian Navy reveals ambitious expansion, indigenisation programme" *India Defence* news report, September 05, 2006 at http://www.india-defence.com/reports/2460 (Accessed 9 Dec 06).
57. 'India wants Maldives as Intelligence Base', *Minivan News*, April 27, 2006 at http://www.minivannews.com/news/news.php?id=2033 (Accessed 01 May 06).
58. 'India activates first listening post on foreign soil: radars in Madagascar', *Indian Express*, New Delhi, July 18, 2007, p. 2.
59. 'India: Court jails pirates in breakthrough for maritime security', Statement issued by International Maritime Bureau (IMB), *Cargo Security International*, March 28, 2003, at http://www.cargosecurityinternational.com/channeldetail.asp?cid=9&caid=853 (Accessed 05 Dec 06).
60. Japan Ministry of Foreign Affairs (MOFA) press release, September 4, 2006 at http://www.mofa.go.jp/announce/announce/2006/9/0904.html and ReCAAP *Information Sharing Centre* website http://www.recaap.org/publish/recaap/index.html (Accessed 9 Dec 06).
61. Ministry of Transport (Singapore) press release, November 20, 2006 at http://app.mot.gov.sg/data/pr_06_11_29.htm (Accessed 9 Dec 06).
62. "Coastguards adopt Amarsective 2004", *The Star*, June 28, 2004 at http://202.186.86.35/maritime/story.asp?file=/2004/6/28/maritime/8288099&sec=maritime (Accessed 26 Dec 06).
63. Ministry of Defence (MoD), Government of India press release, June 3, 2006, at http://pib.nic.in/release/release.asp?relid=18213 (Accessed 26 Dec 06).
64. 'US sees greater Indian role in Malacca Straits', *India eNews*, May 23rd, 2006 at http://indiaenews.com/2006-05/8872-sees-greater-indian-role-malacca-straits.htm (Accessed 08 Oct 06).
65. Rezaul H. Laskar, 'No problem if India patrols regional waters: Chinese envoy', *New Kerela* online, October 28, 2005 at http://www.newkerala.com/news.php?action=fullnews&id=43186 (Accessed 07 Feb 06).

66. Based on the author's informal interactions with Japanese security analysts at the Track-Two level.
67. The forum is modelled on the highly successful *Shangri La* Dialogue. The other stake-holders were Australia, France, Germany, Japan, Pakistan, Russia, Singapore and the UK. The Indian delegation was led by NSA, with the C-in-C of India's Eastern Naval Command participating in maritime-security deliberations. "*The Manama Dialogue*: The Third IISS Regional Security Summit', *IISS* Newsletter, Winter 2006, p. 5, at http://www.iiss.org/conferences/the-iiss-regional-security-summit (01 Feb 07).
68. For details on applicability of PSI and CSI to India, see Gurpreet S Khurana, 'Maritime Non-Proliferation Initiatives: India's Bulwarks Against Nuclear Terrorism?', *Emerging Nuclear Proliferation Challenges*, C Uday Bhaskar and C Raja Mohan (ed.), IDSA-Pugwash India, New Delhi, April 2005, p. 101-118.
69. The cargo manifest had stated that it was carrying "sugar" and "water-refining equipment". Government of India press-release, July 10, 1999, New Delhi, at http://www.indianembassy.org/pic/PR_1999/July_1999/PR_July_10_1999.html (Accessed 05 Aug 07).
70. 'Korean ship mystery', *The Telegraph* (Calcutta), November 10, 2006, at http://www.telegraphindia.com/1061110/asp/nation/story_6981543.asp (Accessed 13 Aug 07).
71. 'How to wave the flag', *Indian Express*, April 20, 2007, p. 8 (editorial page).
72. 'A more secure world: Our shared responsibility', Report of the Secretary General's High-level Panel on Threats, Challenges and Change, *United Nations*, 2004, p. 45.
73. The legality of 'Anticipatory self-defense' has a historical foundation in the *Caroline case* of 1841. During the armed rebellion in Canada against Britain in 1837, the British forces entered US territory to destroy a ship called *Caroline* suspected of providing supplies to the Canadian insurgents. Two US citizens were also killed in the attack. The ensuing correspondence between US Secretary of State and British officials has thence began to be acknowledged as customary international law. It stated, "It will be for ...(Her

Majesty's) Government to show a necessity of self-defence, instant, overwhelming, leaving no choice of means, and no moment for deliberation. It will be for it to show, also, that the local authorities of Canada, even supposing the necessity of the moment authorized them to enter the territories of the US at all, did nothing unreasonable or excessive; since the act, justified by the necessity of self-defence, must be limited by that necessity, and kept clearly within it." This correspondence occurred between Mr. Daniel Webster, the US Secretary of State and Mr. Fox of the UK in April 24, 1841. See, DH Joyner, '*The PSI and International Law*', The Monitor, Spring 2004, Vol. 10, No. 1, pp. 7-9, at http://www.uga.edu/cits/documents/pdf/monitor/monitor_sp_2004.pdf (Accessed 13 Aug 07).

74. Text of UN Security Council Resolution 1540 (2004), April 28, 2004, at http://www.state.gov/documents/organization/32097.pdf (Accessed 16 Aug 07).
75. 'Navy to get 8 vessels for detecting mines', *Times of India*, January 9, 2006, p. 13.
76. Vivek Raghuvanshi, 'Leased Akulas Advance India's Blue-Water Plans', *Defence News*, March 5, 2007, p. 1 and p. 22.
77. The *Prithvil Dhanush* nuclear-capable ballistic missile reported to be inducted by the Navy for its *Sukanya*-class offshore patrol vessels is only a 'technology demonstrator'. See, Rajat Pandit, 'Navy, IAF induct Prithvi', *Times of India*, August 22, 2006, p. 12.
78. ibid.
79. Syed Ali Mujtaba, 'Burmese naval chief meets India 's military brass', *Mizzima News*, April 3, 2007, athttp://www.mizzima.com/MizzimaNews/News/2007/April/05-Apr-2007.html (Accessed 04 Apr 07).
80. 'Indian warships to ensure security to African summit', *Times of India*, July 4, 2003 at http://timesofindia.indiatimes.com/articleshow/60159.cms and Sudha Ramachandran, 'Maldives: Tiny islands, big intrigue', *Asia Times* online, April 7, 2006, at http://www.atimes.com/atimes/South_Asia/HD07Df01.html and 'India to assist Mauritius in hydrographic survey', Indian Navy press release, October 24, 2005 at http://indiannavy.nic.in/press%202005/pres95.htm (All accessed 05 Apr 07).

81. 'Spare parts for Vietnam', *The Tribune*, June 11, 2005, at http://www.tribuneindia.com/2005/20050611/edit.htm (Accessed 05 Apr 07).
82. 'India transfers naval patrol craft to Maldives' (November 21, 2005) and 'Transfer of an Indian naval patrol craft to Seychelles' (15 February, 2005), Indian Navy press releases, at http://indiannavy.nic.in/press05.htm (Accessed 05 Apr 07).
83. The operation followed thereafter in quick succession. While the first IL-76 reached Indonesia on 29 May, the first ship INS Rajput (diverted from another mission) reached by the evening of the following day. Information sourced from IDSA records.
84. Rajat Pandit, 'Navy uses wargames to win allies', *Times of India*, March 30, 2007, p. 13.
85. Rajat Pandit, 'Navy set for wargames on foreign shores', *Times of India*, December 5, 2006, p. 14.
86. Colonel Anil Shorey, 'The Naval Saga in Somalia', *Ministry of Defence* (*Government of India*) website, March 1, 2006, at http://www.mod.nic.in/samachar/march1-06/h2.htm (Accessed 05 Apr 07).
87. 'Second US carrier arrives off Iran', Herald Sun, February 20, 2007, at http://www.news.com.au/heraldsun/story/0,21985,21259590-5005961,00.html (Accessed 05 Apr 07).
88. Vice Admiral (Retd.) GM Hiranandani. *Transition to Eminence – The Indian Navy 1976-1990.* (Lancer Publishers, New Delhi, 2005), p. 195 and 242.
89. 'Navy vessel rescues stranded Indian sailors in Seychelles', *The Hindu*, April 12, 2006 at http://www.hindu.com/2006/04/12/stories/2006041210381500.htm (Accessed 05 May 06).
90. The evacuation of other nationals is another significant example of the navy's politico-diplomatic role. 'Operation *Sukoon* for the evacuation of Indian nationals from Lebanon', Ministry of Defence (Govt. of India) press release, August 24, 2006, at http://pib.nic.in/release/release.asp?relid=20224 (Accessed 05 Apr 07).
91. Sutirtho Patranobis, 'Navy ready, waiting to go', *Hindustan Times*, March 10, 2006, p. 1.
92. Data collated by author from Integrated Headquarters MoD (Navy) sources and placed in IDSA records (Operation *Sukoon* Time-line).

Conclusion

There is little contention that the significance of naval power is increasing in the current times. This is broadly driven by the emerging global geo-political and security environment, which continues to be in a state of flux. More specifically, this is a consequence of four factors. The *foremost* among these is the prevailing security challenge that nations presently encounter. Added to persisting military insecurities, which states need to respond to through credible deterrence, the rapidly proliferating non-state violence and disorder at sea is making naval forces increasingly relevant due to their non-military employment in constabulary, benign and diplomatic roles.

Secondly, most naval missions are closely linked to a state's economic growth. As economics has become a focus of the current globalisation trends, naval power has assumed greater salience. Liked to this is the growth of state's other 'soft' interests in maritime domain, which is becoming increasingly important as the source of mineral resources for industrial development and living resources for nations' long-term food security. Naval forces may thus be called upon increasingly to secure the country's developmental/economic interests overseas, which may or may not be 'maritime' in nature.

Thirdly, naval power also becomes essential to further a vital national interest of human security, not only in terms of the safety of seafarers, fishermen and others involved in scientific and economic activity at sea, but also, as in Indian context, the security and well-being of Indian nationals abroad, who constitute a valuable national resource.

Lastly, given the increasing global focus on security of maritime realm, naval power has become a key element of state power and a currency of influence in international relations. Its potential to be used as a diplomatic instrument has, therefore, increased today, which could bear dividends that transcend the military sphere into political, economic, technological, and other domains.

Given New Delhi's growing political eminence in global affairs and its expanding 'vital' and 'important' interests overseas, the aforesaid is most applicable in Indian context. This may, therefore, necessitate appropriate policies, such as with regard to the (re-) orientation of the capabilities of Indian maritime forces and forging cooperative security bonds with other countries. However, there would inevitably be impediments along the way, which could be grouped under three broad categories – domestic politics, financial or simply, a resistance to change.

The strengthening of military ties with major powers could be perceived by some political sections as being against India's long standing ideological position of "non-alignment". This could be easily used by dissident political groups in India to further their vested interests by impeding government policy-making. At times, the Central government leadership may be thoroughly convinced that a particular policy is in the best interest of the nation, and yet unable to implement it due to a political discord with the concerned (provincial) state governments.

The capacity building of maritime forces is likely to be

more severely constrained by limitations of monetary allocation for modernisation. To some measure, this is due to the intensity of 'guns versus butter' debates in a multi-party democracy like India, and the lack of realisation that making maritime forces capable would not stymie the nation's socio-economic development, but is rather catalyze the process. It must be conceded however that it is largely due to the compulsions of national development, that sufficient resources are unlikely to be allocated to the Indian maritime forces (as to the other Armed Forces). The forces will therefore need to prioritize their requirements, while also drawing up time-lines to achieve them.

Broadly, the *most immediate* need is to develop the marine police of coastal states and the Coast Guard to relieve the Navy of constabulary tasks in the maritime zones (while maintaining the optimum 'overlap'). Concurrently, it is imperative to achieve maritime domain awareness (MDA), not only up to the farthest extremes of India's maritime zones, but also beyond, at least commensurate with the desired naval reach. It may be worthy of noting that although MDA is the most essential prerequisite for any maritime operation, it is an 'intangible' capability. This need may therefore tend to be overlooked during the allocation of scarce resources for modernization, since the process often tends to achieve 'more *bang* for the *buck*'.

In the *short-to-medium-term timeframe*, the Navy will need to expand MDA to the underwater domain in vicinity of India's littoral VAs/VPs and critical choke-points by deploying appropriate sensors, while also developing 'hard-kill' against sub-surface threats that are likely to abound in its waters by that time. The threat will also necessitate a defence against advanced submarine-launched anti-ship and land-attack missiles. During this period, India could steadily augment its integral sealift and airlift capacity for amphibious and OOA operations through induction of indigenous LPDs, while also earmarking and training commensurate rapid-response forces.

In the *medium-to-long-term*, India's naval forces will need to possess the ability to project power overseas. In the least, this will necessitate a reach of its integral carrier-borne air-power to the extremities of Indian Ocean, and nuclear submarines with land-attack capability up to the nearest shores of adjoining oceans

The most overwhelming hurdle to New Delhi's utilization of its maritime forces to secure national interests is posed by the resistance to 'change', either due to ignorance of 'matters-maritime' or simply a psychological 'static inertia'. As a result, India's policy 'realignments' in the past have often been marked by a characteristic what physicists would call, "high specific-heat" – profoundly measured and deliberate, but too slow. It was therefore not surprising that in wake of the Indo-US Defence Agreement of July 2005, the then Indian Naval Chief, Admiral Arun Prakash described in lighter vein the "apprehensions in the media that we (India) had sold something – either our sovereignty or the Indian Ocean!"[1] Closely connected to this is India's traditional continental mindset, which would need to be altered to a maritime-oriented one that looks beyond confines of South Asia. This will concomitantly lead to development of a strategic culture, the absence of which is palpable.[2] This will also bring forth a political culture, which sheds a traditional reticence to acquire and use military power to further its interests. The aforesaid however can only follow and not precede the awareness of the true potential of naval power to further national interests, which has applications much beyond affairs of the sea.

REFERENCES

1. Address by Admiral Arun Prakash (the then Indian Naval Chief) at *United Services Institution* (USI) on the 2nd anniversary of *Force* news-magazine, New Delhi, July 22, 2005.
2. Subhash Kapila, 'India's National Security Council: A Critical Review', *South Asia Analyses Group* (SAAG) paper, May 10, 2000, at http://www.saag.org/papers2/paper123.html (Accessed 05 Apr 07).

Index